# How to Manage Your Workforce in the Digital Age

COLIN BEAMES

© 2019 Colin Beames
Published in 2019 by Advanced Workforce Strategies Pty Ltd
advancedworkforcestrategies.com

Design by Natalie Tunstill & Andrew Tesdorpf

Printed in Australia

No part of this book may be reproduced, stored in a retrieval system, or transmitted by any means without the written permission of the author.

| | Preface | 7 |
|---|---|---|
| **1.** | **Technological Developments & Digital Disruption** | **11** |
| 1.1 | The 4th Industrial Revolution (4IR) | 12 |
| 1.2 | More About Technology Advancements | 16 |
| 1.3 | Business & Digital Disruption | 18 |
| 1.4 | Causes of Digital Disruption | 21 |
| **2.** | **Innovation** | **29** |
| 2.1 | Innovation: What it Really Means | 30 |
| 2.2 | Innovation Centres & Digital Strategy | 32 |
| **3.** | **Three Other Current Trends Impacting on the Workplace & Workers** | **37** |
| 3.1 | The Changing Nature of Work & Workers | 38 |
| 3.2 | Longevity & the Ageing Workforce | 38 |
| 3.3 | Lower Growth Economy | 40 |
| 3.4 | Changing Family Structures | 41 |
| 3.5 | Other Recent Past Workplace & Workforce Developments | 41 |
| **4.** | **The Impact on Organisations, Jobs and People** | **43** |
| 4.1 | The Impact on Organisations | 44 |
| 4.2 | The Impact on Jobs | 45 |
| 4.3 | Borderless Working | 52 |
| 4.4 | Flexible Work Practices | 54 |
| 4.5 | Growth of the Extended Workforce & Talent Management Strategies | 57 |
| 4.6 | Careers | 59 |
| 4.7 | Learning | 61 |
| 4.8 | Organisational Design | 69 |
| 4.9 | Leadership | 81 |
| 4.10 | Culture | 86 |
| 4.11 | People Management Practices in Digital Organisations | 89 |
| 4.12 | The Agile Organisation | 94 |
| **5.** | **Digital Transformation** | **103** |
| 5.1 | Digital: The New Way of Doing Things | 104 |
| 5.2 | What is Digital Transformation? | 105 |
| 5.3 | The Goals of Digital Transformation | 106 |
| 5.4 | Impacts of Digital Transformation | 106 |

| 5.5 | Digital Transformation Isn't Cheap | 108 |
| --- | --- | --- |
| 5.6 | Phases of Digitisation | 108 |
| 5.7 | Five Levels of Digital Transformation | 109 |
| 5.8 | Platform Ecosystems, the Cloud & Digital Transformation | 112 |
| 5.9 | Mastering Digital Customer Experience & Operational Excellence | 113 |
| 5.10 | Going Digital Is a 'Mixed Bag' | 114 |
| 5.11 | The Challenges of Going Digital | 115 |
| 5.12 | Approaches to Going Digital | 119 |
| **6.** | **The Nine Key Steps in Digital Transformation** | **121** |
| 6.1 | The Nine Key Steps in Digital Transformation | 122 |
| 6.2 | Step 1: Implement a Governance & Project Management Structure | 123 |
| 6.3 | Step 2: Develop the New Proposed Business & Digital Strategy & Associated Business Model | 125 |
| 6.4 | Step 3: Define the New Processes & Design, Build & Deploy the New Digital Platform & Infrastructure | 129 |
| 6.5 | Step 4: Develop a Transition or Change Plan | 130 |
| 6.6 | Step 5: Identify the Legacy Workforce Blueprint | 131 |
| 6.7 | Step 6: Design the New Organisational Structure | 134 |
| 6.8 | Step 7: Identify the Required Actions to Establish the New Workforce Configuration | 137 |
| 6.9 | Step 8: Develop a Digital Culture, Digital Workforce & Digital Workplace | 139 |
| 6.10 | Step 9: Implement Controls to Monitor & Optimise Business Processes & Outcomes | 145 |
| **7.** | **Two Key Extended Roles in Digital Transformation** | **145** |
| 7.1 | Two Key Extended Roles | 148 |
| 7.2 | The Role of the CIO | 148 |
| 7.3 | The Role of the HR Director/Manager | 150 |
| **8.** | **Developing a Digital Workplace Strategy** | **155** |
| 8.1 | Communications Are Critical in the Digital Economy | 156 |
| 8.2 | HR Technology in the Digital Workplace | 157 |
| **9.** | **Technology & HR Analytics** | **161** |
| 9.1 | HR Analytics Now a Business Discipline | 162 |
| 9.2 | Ownership of HR Analytics | 163 |
| 9.3 | Strategy Before HR Analytics | 163 |
| 9.4 | Some Definitions: Metrics, Measures, Data & Analytics | 164 |

| | | |
|---|---|---|
| 9.5 | Investment in HR Technology | 166 |
| 9.6 | Implementing HR Analytics | 172 |
| **10.** | **Conclusions** | **176** |
| **References** | | **177** |

**Appendix A: Other Recent Past Workplace & Workforce Developments** — **181**

| | | |
|---|---|---|
| A.1 | Recent Workplace Changes | 182 |
| A.2 | New Meanings in the Workplace | 184 |
| A.3 | Organisational & People Management Trends | 185 |
| A.4 | Changing Employment Practices | 186 |
| A.5 | The 'Old Deal' & the 'New Deal' | 188 |
| A.6 | 'New Deal' Implications | 190 |
| A.7 | Workforce Diversity & Three Generations | 191 |
| A.8 | Overall Implications & Challenges for Organisations | 197 |
| A.9 | Overall Implications & Challenges for Individuals | 198 |

**Appendix B: Stages of Life** — **199**

| | | |
|---|---|---|
| B.1 | Erikson's Stages of Life | 200 |
| B.2 | Jung's Theory of Individuation | 201 |

**Appendix C: Careers in the Contemporary Workplace** — **203**

| | | |
|---|---|---|
| C.1 | The Traditional Career Model | 204 |
| C.2 | New Career Models | 205 |
| C.3 | Implications of New Career Models for Employees | 206 |
| C.4 | The New Worker & Careers | 207 |
| C.5 | Implications of New Career Models for Organisations | 210 |
| C.6 | Implications of New Career Models for Managers | 211 |

**Appendix D: The AWS Skills-Based Workforce Segmentation Model, Questionnaire & Plotting Tool** — **213**

| | | |
|---|---|---|
| D.1 | About Critical Roles | 214 |
| D.2 | About the Skills Segmentation Questionnaire (SSQ) | 216 |
| D.3 | Analysing and Plotting Roles | 219 |

**Appendix E: Aligning Workforce and Business Strategies** — **223**

**About the Author** — **226**

**Client Testimonials** — **228**

# Preface

Up until recently Strategic Workforce Planning has been a latent need for most organisations. The importance of strategically managing an organisation's most vital intangible asset—its people—has not been adequately recognised or appreciated by Boards, Executives and HR professionals alike. The people factor is typically the largest cost item in the budget (i.e., labour), and the largest driver of business outcomes. This lack of recognition is a result of a number of factors including:

- Many CEOs coming from a financial background with little understanding of the importance of the people factor, and its impact on business outcomes;
- The lack of a business focus and influence of some Human Resources (HR) professionals, including the capability to argue the business case for the development of a Strategic Workforce Plan;
- The continuing evolution or emergence of strategic Human Resources as opposed to the administrative HR function;
- A general lack of understanding as to what Strategic Workforce Planning is, and how it differs significantly from Workforce Planning.

Now all of this is changing or about to change, with the key driver of this change emerging from the advent of the 4th Industrial Revolution (4IR), including developments in technology and digital disruption, all of which are affecting business models, work practices and employees' life styles.

Changes to the business model means changes to the shape of the workforce. It is mission-critical to anticipate how changing strategies and business models will alter an organisation's workforce requirements. Hence the imperative is to adopt a more strategic approach to workforce management:

- Starting with an understanding of the legacy (existing) workforce;
- Then identifying the new processes, organisational structures, skills and capability requirements; and
- Ultimately transitioning to the new workforce configuration.

Apart from technological developments, digital disruption and the changing nature of work, other drivers of the need for Strategic Workforce Planning include:

- The need to improve productivity/efficiency and remain competitive;
- A low growth economy, at least in the medium term;
- Increased competition for top talent;
- The need to mitigate risk;
- Borderless working and the rising demand for flexible work arrangements;
- The changing nature of the worker, becoming more age diverse, more ethnic diverse, more mobile and more autonomous;
- The changing expectations of customers in ways that are more relevant to user demands;
- Changing workforce demographics, including an ageing workforce and changing family structures.

Thus the application of Strategic Workforce Planning is now a key emerging issue, becoming 'front and centre' in the new economy. However many organisations are grappling to understand and address the challenges of workforce reconfiguration against the background of these emerging changes. There is very little precedent as to how best to tackle this challenge. Many organisations are, or will be, entering uncharted waters. Some are faced with enacting a parallel (or two speed) organisation, which is dynamic enough to transact today, as well as build for the future.

HR and IT, previously back office functions, are now both in the 'eye of the storm'—their close collaboration is vital to successful transformation. More specifically HR has a key role to play—both as a passenger and a driver—in building a digital culture, workplace and workforce.

To that end this book is designed to assist executives and HR professionals in navigating the digital journey. Even for those organisations less affected by digital disruption, they will find the book relevant in how they best manage their workforce. It provides an over view of the digital world, workplace trends, digital disruption, digital workforce transformation, and the extended role of the CIO and HR Director/Manager.

*Colin Beames*

Chapter 1

# Technological Developments & Digital Disruption

# 1.1 The 4th Industrial Revolution (4IR)

## A Brief History of Industrial Revolutions

The first Industrial Revolution (1IR) occurred in the period from about 1760 to sometime between 1820 and 1840 with a transition to new manufacturing processes, utilising water and steam power to mechanise production.

The second Industrial Revolution (2IR) came about in the early 20th century, when Henry Ford mastered the moving assembly line and ushered in the age of mass production using electric power. The first two industrial revolutions made people richer and more urban.

The third Industrial Revolution (3IR) only emerged relatively recently (i.e., in the last 40–50 years) with manufacturing going digital, using electronics and information technology to automate production.

When science and technology meet social and economic systems, then something akin to what the late Stephen Jay Could called 'punctuated equilibrium' occurs in his description of evolutionary biology. Something that has been stable for a long period is suddenly disrupted radically – and then settles into a new equilibrium. Each of these innovations collided with society that had been in a period of relative stasis – followed by massive disruption.

Now a Fourth Industrial Revolution (4IR) is building on the Third.

*A 4IR definition: The fusion of technologies that are blurring the lines between the physical, digital and biological spheres.*

It may seem like the 3IR and 4IR are too close together, however that is probably the point. The world of business has changed dramatically in only a 50 year period, so imagine how much it will change in a truly digital age.

## The Defining Characteristics of 4IR

There are three reasons why today's transformations represent not merely a prolongation of the 3IR, but rather the arrival of a Fourth and distinct one:

1. Velocity
2. Scope
3. Systems impact.

The speed of current breakthroughs has no historical precedent. When compared with previous Industrial Revolutions, the Fourth is evolving at an exponential rather than at a linear pace. Moreover, it is disrupting almost every industry in every country with the breadth and depth of these changes, heralding the transformation of entire systems of production, management, and governance.

## The 4IR and Future Technologies

The 4IR is just about upon us. We are basking in the dawn of the rise of algorithms, automation, cognitive technologies including machine learning and Artificial Intelligence (AI), all of which are altering the trajectory of global economies, labour markets and corporate growth strategies. The possibilities of billions of people connected by mobile devices with unprecedented processing power, storage capacity and access to knowledge, are unlimited. And these possibilities will be multiplied by emerging technology breakthroughs in the fields listed below.

These emerging 12 future technologies underpinning the 4IR will transfer the world in many ways—some desirably and others may argue some undesirably.

### 1. 3D Printing

Bioprinting of organic tissues is already being used for drug testing. Printed body parts are expected to be available within a few years. Clothes, especially shoes, are already being printed for the perfect fit.

### 2. Nanotechnology

The application of atomic or nanoscale materials will continue to expand as new materials are created for their thermoelectricity efficiency and shape retention. Nanotechnology will include energy producing clothing to power our personal gadgets and biological sensors to monitor our health.

### 3. Space Technologies

Space technological developments will allow for greater access to and exploration of space, including microsatellites, advanced telescopes, reusable rockets, and integrated rocket-jet engines.

### 4. Energy Capture and Storage Transmission

Breakthroughs in battery storage and fuel cell efficiency will enable capturing of renewable energy through solar, wind, and tidal technologies, with energy distribution through smart grid systems and wireless energy transfer.

### 5. Biotechnologies

Biotechnologies Include capital advances in genetic engineering, resequencing and therapeutics, as well as human-computational interfaces and synthetic biology.

### 6. Automation, Artificial Intelligence and Robots

Automation aims to eliminate or minimise human interaction in a process. Machines that can substitute for humans are being increasingly being used in tasks associated with thinking, multitasking and fine motor skills.

> *Artificial Intelligence (AI) is a computer science that uses machine learning algorithms designed to mimic human cognitive functions.*

AI aims to replicate the structure of the brain itself, using the concept of neural networks to form vast webs of interconnected pathways, capable not only of immense and complex processing, but also of adaptive learning. This means more and more, machines will become more autonomous.

### 7. Neurotechnologies

Neurotechnologies include smart drugs, neuroimaging and biotechology interfaces that allow for reading, communicating, and influencing human brain activity.

## 8. Virtual and Augmented Realities

Virtual and augmented realities include next-step interfaces between humans and computers, involving immersive environments, holographic readouts and digitally produced overlays for mixed-reality experiences.

## 9. Ubiquitous and Linked Sensors

Networked electronic sensors are being used to connect, track, and manage remote products, systems and grids, providing new or better quality information, and offering new possibilities for regulation and control. People will leave a digital trail wherever they go with connected sensors.

## 10. Blockchain and Distributed Ledger Technology

Distributed ledger technology (secure synchronised digital data spread across multiple sites) is already being trialled by banks based on blockchains that are inherently resistant to retro modification of data. This is the basis of 'cryptocurrencies' such as bitcoin.

## 11. Advanced Computer Technologies

Advanced computer technologies include:

- Quantum computing (harvesting the power of atoms and molecules to perform super fast memory and processing tasks);
- Biological computing (using biological derived materials such as DNA to perform computational functions); and
- Natural network processing (processing information in a dynamic way resembling the human brain).

## 12. Geoengineering

Geoengineering includes technological interventions in planetary systems, typically to mitigate the effects of climate change by removing carbon dioxide from the atmosphere or managing solar radiation.

How quickly these technologies start to manifest themselves is yet to be played out, including their cultural and economic impacts.

## Multiple Technologies

Most radical technological advancements come not from linear improvements within a field of expertise, but from the combination of seemingly disparate connections and disciplines. Multiple technologies can be combined in different ways in transforming the world. There is a pattern of one technology giving rise to the next with the real value coming from how they combine to create new synergies. Glimpses into the future that combine some of the above technologies include, for example, driverless vehicles that may reduce or eliminate car ownership and accidents. Roads will be freed up cutting insurance rates to threads. Driverless cars will also offer a new functionality, providing places to work, or to be entertained, or to have meetings, etc.

The 4IR is a digital revolution that is forcing a fundamental transformation of business. It will reshape business strategies, reshape companies, disrupt business, create performance and productivity opportunities for business and the economy, and reshape employment and the future of work. We are experiencing disruption of our world of work as a result of this tectonic shift that is just as dramatic as industrialisation and urbanisation.

# 1.2 More About Technology Advancements

## Technology, Innovation and Competition

As referred to above, technology advancements are transforming products, channels and operations leading to an extraordinary rate of innovation in products and services. New sources of competitive pressure have been created with enormous potential for future growth, profitability and cost reduction emerging. Business and government are experiencing rapid changes in the marketplace requiring a basic rethink of their business model and continuous adaptation in strategy, decision-making and action.

The global stage is in a state of perpetual motion with multi-polarisation, where the competition is coming from here, there and everywhere. Technology has improved accessibility and has usurped geography! We now live in a truly connected world through inexpensive mobile devices with personal interfaces.

Globalisation has progressed to global interconnectedness, where not only goods but also information and ideas, flow across borders constantly and freely with near universal access to the internet. These communications accelerate ideation and product development.

## The Internet of Things (IoT)

*Wikipedia defines The Internet of Things (IoT) as: The inter-networking of physical devices, vehicles (also referred to as 'connected devices' and 'smart devices'), buildings, and other items—embedded with electronics, software, sensors, actuators, and network connectivity that enable these objects to collect and exchange data.*

The IoT is a new way of gathering facts, including new facts, moving from assumption to information through to understanding. It combines data with people, processes and things. The use of data and analytics enables:

- Faster and larger-scale evidence based decisions;
- Insight generation; and
- Process optimisation.

*Data is the new oil of the century.*

Data-driven approaches are reshaping some industries by identifying:

- Inefficient matching of supply and demand;
- Prevalence of under utilised assets;
- Behavioural data obviating the need for dependence on large amount of demographic data; and
- Human biases and errors in a data-rich environment.

Data is thus changing how we think and act with businesses facing an explosion of data to exploit.

## The Cloud

> *The term 'cloud' refers to the software and services that run on the internet and not on a computer's hard drive. It is a vast network of computer services that are stored all over the world.*

The cloud acts like a giant utility in the sky to store, access, and share data from internet-connected services. It is not related to the weather and it is not some nebulous mass holding data. Rather it's just someone else's computer!

Information that is stored in the cloud can be accessed from anywhere. It amplifies growing technologies individually and collectively. It creates a tremendous release of energy into the hands of individuals to compete, design, think, imagine, connect and collaborate with anyone, anywhere. The cloud is enabling the reshaping of every man-made system that modern society is built on. Everything is being changed and everything is being impacted upon, both positively and negatively.

## 1.3 Business & Digital Disruption

> *Digital businesses are those that win, serve, and retain customers by continuously creating and exploiting digital assets to simultaneously deliver new sources of customer value and increase their operational agility.*
>
> *Disruption: A disturbance or a problem that interrupts an event, activity or process.*

### Disrupt or be Disrupted!

The digital genie is out of the bottle. Digitisation is the new universe—it is the new way of doing things. The digital revolution is a function of business evolution and technology. Digitisation and the nascent IoT are enabling digital-first companies to challenge traditional business models. These companies (i.e., digital disruptors) are a direct threat to established market leaders and prevailing economic structures. We have entered an age of perpetual instability in business and society where the new mantra is 'disrupt or be disrupted'. This poses a clear challenge to legacy businesses: adapt or die!

Digital reduces barriers to entry, blurs category boundaries, opens doors for a new generation of entrepreneurs and innovators, and in turn, incumbent market leaders will face substantial pressures. It drives instant delivery and zero marginal cost with flawless ability to connect people, devices, and physical objects anywhere. It is a profound force in our economy, changing the very nature of consumption, competition, how markets work and the relationships that put consumers and other individuals in the drivers' seat.

## Extent of Digital Disruption

*A recent Merryck study (cited in Reimer, Feuerstein, Meighan & Kelly, 2017) of global talent leaders and CHROs confirmed 85% of companies are wrestling with a shift in their business model, with these shifts including: navigating the cloud, integrating a digital strategy, incorporating some elements of AI, building an enterprise mindset across the matrix, and increasing the velocity of execution and strategy adjustments.*

In a recent survey, 90% of 1,000 business leaders surveyed believed their core business is threatened by new digital competitors that are challenging their products and services (Kane, Palmer, Phillips, Kiron & Buckley, 2016). Executives are asking themselves: *Will we be Uber-ed?* They are concerned that a failure to understand and act on digitisation will leave them vulnerable to digital disruption.

Some of Australia's most iconic business brands are under threat with one third of the Australian economy facing imminent and substantial disruption by digital technologies and business models—what Deloitte (2017) refers to as a 'short fuse, big bang' scenario. This presents significant threats, as well as opportunities for both business and government. For some, digital disruption will be immediate and explosive—a force that rocks the foundations of their business. For others less vulnerable to digital disruption, the changes will be slower and more subtle. And yet for others, digital innovation will be the cornerstone of future value creation.

According to Deloitte, industry sectors that have a short fuse include: finance, retail, media and information, communications technology. Those industry sectors reported to have a longer fuse include: education and health.

## Survival Isn't a Given!

Survival isn't a given! No industry is immune to the changes brought by digital disruption. The things that used to set companies apart — such as economies of scale, distribution strength, and brand — are far less potent than they used to be. Now many customers, products, business operations, and competitors are fundamentally digital. The basic rules of the game for creating and capturing economic value, that once were fixed, are now subject to rapid displacement, disruption and in some cases destruction. Digital renders intermediaries obsolete, and drives marginal costs to almost zero.

Fifty years ago, the average life span of a Fortune 500 company was around 75 years (Perry, 2014). Today it is less than 15 years and getting shorter. More and more, incremental growth and business improvement are no longer valued or celebrated. The growth curve has taken an exponential upwards turn.

However too few companies are facing up to the challenge of digital transformation, either lacking in digital leadership, and/or familiarity with the processes and benefits. A failure to learn, innovate and create can see people at the top of their game quickly outpaced.

*Note. Apart from the universities and the churches, very few organisations have stood the test of time and survived for more than a century.*

## Reactions to Disruption

Some business leaders haven't thought of digital as central to their business because in the past it hasn't been. Very few have a broad holistic view as to what digital means. Differing views on disruption or reactions to digital disruption include the following:

- Disruption for disruption's sake, hoping that this is a passing phase and that things will eventually return to normal;
- A natural consequence of our age of increasing complexity, pushing from the outside, forcing organisations to change their business models and service offerings (which forces leaders to be defensive in their reaction in the face of accelerating changes to business and society, a reactionary response based on risk and fear);
- Enables businesses to build a future oriented organisation, needing to transcend disruption, posing questions such as the following:
    - What opportunities are yet to be recognised?

- How can the organisation move beyond its present capabilities?
- How can the organisation better connect with its customers including understanding their ecosystems?

In terms of the latter, a multi-faceted strategy (i.e., with various options) is suggested given the future unknowns, with one of the keys being the identification of the organisation's higher purpose (apart from the need to be profitable). Furthermore, the unbundling of current products and services may uncover or present a focus on new core businesses.

## 1.4 Causes of Digital Disruption

*Digital disruption is mainly used in the sense that an industry, way of doing business or ecosystem (e.g. societal) is significantly challenged by existing (mostly tech) companies, newcomers or incumbents who have mastered digital business skillsets and came up with solutions, business models and approaches that cause a significant shift in customer behaviour and market context, requiring existing players (which can include 'digital businesses') to change their strategies as well (CIO, 2017).*

Disruption is the catalyst for new ways to think about and solve problems. Apart from affecting business models, digital disruption is also affecting work practices and employees' lifestyles. Causes of digital disruption include:

1. Technological innovations (technology-induced), with its use and adoption by customers, partners, competitors and various stakeholders
2. Customer behaviour and demands, seeking ease of use and simplicity
3. Innovation and invention-induced, as referred to earlier in the 12 emerging technologies that underpin the 4IR
4. Ecosystem-induced, including economical changes, demands from partners who want parties to adapt, regulatory changes, geo-political changes, etc.

These four disruption causes are elaborated upon below.

## 1. Technology-Induced Innovations

Technology is a strategic enabler with technology induced disruptive business models popping up everywhere. These business models are leveraging digital technology, examples of which include the following:

- Google has disrupted online search and advertising;
- Salesforce has disrupted Customer Relationship Management (CRM);
- Amazon has disrupted retail and distribution by becoming customer obsessive;
- Uber has disrupted transportation becoming the world's largest taxi company that owns no vehicles;
- Airbnb has disrupted accommodation becoming the world's largest accommodation provider that owns no real estate;
- Facebook has disrupted social experiences becoming the world's most popular media provider that creates no content;
- PayPal has disrupted financial services;
- Netflix has disrupted media and entertainment being the world's largest movie house that owns no cinemas;
- Skype has disrupted telecommunications.

These technology-enabled entrants have mastered the software interfaces that connect various goods and services to the masses, and have catered for profound shifts in consumer behaviour. Some of these entrants have inflicted margin erosion, as digital disruptors often target pieces of the value chain and chip away at an incumbent's position.

These disruptors are attacks from outside of the industry. Uber and Airbnb are examples of 'demand side' disruption that only involves the way customers buy products. These companies didn't dramatically change the nature of taxi or hotel services (although they would argue that they provide a more personalised and friendly service). They only changed the way consumers buy and access those services. Access has usurped ownership in their business models. They have tapped previously inaccessible sources of supply to bring to the market a supply chain digital strategy.

Now we are entering a more complex phase known as 'supply side' disruption, which requires businesses to change the way:

- They create and develop products and services; and
- Their people work together, how they build teams, and how they structure incentives so they lead to the best possible outcomes.

This latter point is explored in Chapters 4 and 8.

As incumbent companies are pinned down by many operational and regulatory constraints, customers and new types of competitors are able to move faster than ever. A growing number of companies are adopting an asset- or capital-light model that enables them to enter a market and scale quickly, without taking the same investment path as incumbent firms. Many of these new firms grow through direct network effects and are more open and modular than incumbents' proprietary and interdependent models.

However all technology is not necessarily good technology. Some concerns are emerging recently by investment analysts about the longer-term sustainability of the Uber and Tesla business models. Both firms have substantial borrowings and are a long way off from being profitable.

## 2. Customer Behaviour and Demands

The digital age is far more than automation, digitization and the use of many technologies that enable e-commerce capabilities. It reflects the new social and economic order that pervades our markets, organisations and societies as a whole. It's about people's desire and ability to participate, influence and be fully involved in their community and work life.

Customers are thus becoming digital beings. They now embrace digital technologies and experiences as a normal part of their lives. Their digital expectations continuously evolve and shape their perceptions of value, and how this value needs to be delivered to them. They increasingly want products and services that adapt to their diverse and specific preferences. They want to interact with the providers of those products and services with less effort or intrusion. This personalisation requires companies to understand customers increasingly more as individuals rather than as part of segments. In summary, customers are simultaneously demanding less complexity and more customisation to their needs.

> *85% of executives say that simplifying the customer experience will be critical to success in their market by 2020 (CEB, 2017).*

Digital fundamentally changes the relationship between businesses and their customers. Digital businesses understand that if they are to win in the age of the customer, they must become customer centric, re-engineering how their businesses create value for their customers. Rather than re-envisioning their businesses as a set of products and services, instead they should conceive their businesses as part of their customers value ecosystem, according to their customers needs and desires.

Success means investing in constantly evolving customer experiences, removing friction in those experiences, and understanding that digital technologies have become fundamental in the desired experiences of their customers. In other words, digital and customer experience strategies need to be tightly linked together.

However to succeed in this age of the customer, building a new fancy website or a mobile app is not enough: every aspect of the business must be transformed. At the heart of this transformation to a digital business is the need to redefine how to create and deliver value for customers. To do this requires businesses to fundamentally rethink their:

- Critical capabilities and core competencies;
- Operating models;
- Business processes;
- Organisational structures;
- Technology;
- Skills; and
- Culture.

> *A firm's ability to create value for its customers will depend on how easily the core capabilities of the organisation can be augmented digitally, and realigned to deliver the outcomes desired by the customer, rather than the products or services traditionally sold.*

The competitive landscape is now being driven by the consumer rather than the enterprise, and also by a labour market that is changing to suit the digital landscape. Traditional customer loyalty is becoming a thing of the past with Gen Y representing close to 50% of the population in the next 5 years (currently 22%). Customers should therefore be placed at the heart of the digital strategy, enabling the individualised and heightened experiences that customers now expect and demand. The challenge is to create a digital-first, customer-centric organisation. Digital businesses must become customer-obsessed and not a product company. Success means investing in constantly evolving customer experiences and understanding that technology has become fundamental to how customers perceive value.

*The Importance of the Customer Experience*

More and more businesses are shifting from product and single transaction sales to service and subscription models. Customer experience is taking on a whole new meaning given this growth and reliance on services-related revenue (i.e., professional services, subscription-based services, service-level agreements, managed services and usage-based contracts). One bad customer experience can send a customer for life to a competitor.

### Customer Experience Research

A study by Schmidt-Subramanian and Stern (2016) found that consumers who rate their experiences as satisfied/very satisfied with the product or service:

- Are five times more likely to stay with the company;
- Are eight times more willing to take up new or future services;
- Cost the company six times less to provide acceptable or good service (satisfied customers don't have problems or complain as much as dissatisfied customers which means the company spends less money);
- Are three times more willing to recommend the company to others.

What drives consumer/customer satisfaction? Consumers rate companies on their level of customer satisfaction taking into account:

- Brand – predominantly relates to reputation in the market;
- Price;
- Product – range of features and choices offered with the product;
- Processes – how easy it is to deal with the company;
- Interaction – range and quality of delivery of the services by the available channels (e.g., phone/contact centre, store/branch, website, app, email, text, social media).

Traditionally companies placed emphasis and efforts towards enhancing the first three elements. However recent research has highlighted the importance of customer service and quality of interactions.

Customers now have a stronger say on what brands and products are purchased than ever before with information available from a number of newly emerging sources including:

- Customer advocacy (e.g., use of social media);
- The rise of 'prosumers' – those who talk about and advocate for brands and products;

**Note.** *Prosumers are active consumers skilled in specific product domains, savvy with social media and know how to gain the attention of buyers.*

- An increase in the range of comparative sites (e.g., Webjet, Trivago, iSelect);
- An increase in the number of review sites influencing consumer behaviour (e.g., TripAdvisor, Trustpilot, Choice).

For high performing service companies, initially there is a requirement for the following customer experience foundations to be in place:

- Having a clear vision;
- Researching customer needs and being externally focused;
- Mapping customer journeys;
- Investing in and delivering actions;
- Leadership buy-in.

***Note***. *Journey mapping is a technique used to track the customer experience including the identification of pain points and friction. It starts from the outside-in, seeking to understand the customer experience ecosystem that the business has created to serve those customers. It requires a more detailed view of the customer including:*

1. *Awareness (pre-enrolment stage), including the need, research, and evaluate*
2. *Join (enrolment stage)*
3. *Consume & Pay (post enrolment stage), including the receipt, use, maintain, and replace*
4. *Contact & inform (after sales service)*

*Then it's a case of connecting this outside-in view to the business capabilities to help those customers achieve their outcome. This connection includes identifying the teams, processes, technologies, data and partners that underpin each customer journey, linking business capability mapping to customer journey mapping. Such a combined picture provides an understanding of how to better serve customers, and to identify those parts of the business that may need to change.*

Furthermore, a customer-centric culture lies at the heart of a high-performing service company. It's the most enduring and distinguishing element to make it unique and the hardest to replicate. A customer culture includes:

- The ways in which people work together to deliver customer outcomes;
- Management practices and processes to deliver customer outcomes;
- Actionable behaviours about what's expected.

## 3. Innovation and Invention-Induced

Such disruptions include entirely novel approaches to human and business challenges, as well as innovations and inventions that create an entirely new reality, whether it's in science, business, or technology. Even a non-technological context of true innovation can be disruptive. Refer to some of the previous 12 technologies that underpin the 4IR, including the invention of new medicines that change healthcare and society, 3D printing, driverless cars. The topic of innovation is elaborated upon in Chapter 2.

## 4. Ecosystem Induced

*An ecosystem is a localised community of living organisms interacting with each other. Business ecosystem refers to cooperative network of partners, suppliers, distributors and customers working together to support new products and satisfy customer needs. They deploy technology, tools of connectivity and collaboration.*
*Personal value ecosystems are the set of digitally connected products and services that individuals combine to help satisfy their needs and desires.*

This ecosystem factor goes to the heart of the essential aspect of digital transformation—the interdependency and interconnectedness of everything. It all overlaps and is connected, from business processes and models, to the flow of information, to business activities, and each single activity of the organisation. A world of ecosystems will consist of highly customer-centric models where users can enjoy an end-to-end experience for a wide range of products and services through a single access gateway, without leaving the ecosystem. In this connected world, the boundaries between industry sectors will continue to blur.

Furthermore, connected businesses create ecosystems made up of networks of people from within and outside of the organisation. Ideas and input come from all sides and segments across all stakeholder groups. These businesses actively collaborate with the outside world including partners and even competitors to help find answers and accelerate delivery of products and services. As well as learning from the outside world, these businesses actively contribute to the wider ecosystem, helping to grow and influence their network of clients, partners and suppliers.

In every type of ecosystem, change produces winners and losers. The more dramatic the change, the more pronounced the consequences. The business and human capital ecosystem is no exception. Access to high quality digital infrastructure, human capital and industry technology ecosystems are critical to success. Platform ecosystems are the foundation for new value creation in the digital economy. Refer to Chapter 5 for further discussion on this topic.

Chapter 2

# Innovation

## 2.1 Innovation: What it Really Means

*Innovation means a new method, idea or product. It is the ability to make an idea a commercial reality, to create something of value that clients/customers will pay for, that satisfies a specific need, whether it's a service, product or experience.*
*Innovation can be categorised as Incremental (continuous or evolutionary) or Breakthrough (radical or revolutionary).*
*Disruption and innovation go hand in hand.*
*It is the change that adds value.*

Innovation is the holy grail of business—it's the quest for enlightenment. It has become the next silver bullet for organisations. The ability to innovate, adapt and respond with agility to consumer demands is a business-critical imperative. However innovation is one of todays' most used and least understood words! It is not just about technology, research or even entrepreneurial skills. Rather it is in the intersection of various fields of expertise where innovation is important.

Innovation includes the managerial, marketing, organisational, social, economic and administrative knowledge and the intellectual and creative capacity required to solve business problems and/or translate new opportunities, ideas, and discoveries into innovation. It no longer happens just in the R&D department and it requires hard work, discipline and rigour. Technology facilitates collaboration and knowledge sharing supports innovation.

The most effective innovation strategies focus on people and talent management practices. Innovation requires risk-taking, entrepreneurial behaviour and an environment of trust so new ideas can be tried and fail. This includes:

- Bringing people together with bundles of skills who think differently, and with a background of different experiences (i.e., heterogeneous employees from diverse backgrounds with fresh perspectives) working together as a highly functioning team;
- Different skills at different stages of a project, including communication, collaboration, critical thinking, application, etc.

The biggest barrier to innovation is the lack of appropriate skills mixing, including skills at an individual level, team level and across organisations (networks). Successful innovation is therefore unlikely to occur without the right mix of talent, ways of working, culture and leadership.

Teams frequently comprise partners, contractors, and freelancers with the workforce of the future structured more around transient project-based roles than continuous job functions. As referred to earlier, connected businesses create ecosystems made up of networks of people from within and outside of the organisation to form multi-disciplinary teams together to deliver on specific projects. Refer later to Chapter 4 on the extended workforce and organisational design.

Innovation can include the move towards:

- Perfecting existing products and services and driving costs down, or enhancing value (i.e., Incremental); and/or
- Creating new products and services (i.e., Breakthrough).

Innovation can span across:

- Offerings – products, product system;
- Configurations – structures, process; and
- Experience – service, channels, customer engagement.

Innovation resides in no particular individual, team, or department: it is a chameleon that can manifest anywhere or nowhere depending upon the conditions and the players. It can happen in an *ad hoc* manner, siloed manner, or become an organisation-wide phenomenon. Ideally frameworks for developing, prioritising and refining ideas and formal processes should be in place to support innovation.

**Note.** *Anti-globalisation sentiment is rising. Declining openness and increased protectionist policies and regimes, threaten to undermine future global prosperity by reducing incentives to innovate.*

## 2.2 Innovation Centres & Digital Strategy

**Innovation and Customer Centricity**

The core of the digital strategy is not solely about technology, but cultivating a culture of customer centricity and innovation. This includes understanding the jobs the customer is trying to do, understanding their needs and wants, and then looking for ways to fulfil that job with a highly contextual, friction-free engaging experience.

**Approaches to Innovation**

> *Open innovation and open business models refers to the opening up of a company's research processes to outside parties in a world of distributed knowledge (Chesbrough, 2011).*

Some companies have set up Innovation Centres or Digital Labs to evolve their digital strategy, including hiring digital experts, challenging them to innovate a business process. This may extend to a series of projects that involve working with start-ups or partners to develop multiple programs (i.e., outsourcing innovation and/or co-innovation). These companies may be looking for some injection of entrepreneurial spirit. Matching small disruptive start-ups with larger corporations opens up unlimited resources externally, including the ability to scale.

> ***Note.*** *The Digital Lab team will comprise a team of experts in fields that may include: virtual reality, augmented reality, mixed reality, machine learning, artificial intelligence, robotic process automation, learning analytics, etc. The Lab operates in partnership with business helping to define what their particular problem really is, and thereafter bringing new applications of emerging technology to life, combing resources and expertise. The process is highly collaborative, developing iterative solutions through an Agile methodology (refer later to Chapter 4.12).*

## Process Digitisation: Zero Based Design

Zero based design of the customer experience ignores everything the organisation has in place and asking: *What would be the best possible customer experience when completing this task?* Then the processes and technology to support the experience can be built. These processes can then be digitised to reduce business costs, improve customer experience and capture value.

Some organisations create a purpose built 'lab' or 'pod' (as referred to above) for a team working on a customer journey in order to insulate it from everyday business demands and free it to focus on delivery. This design approach requires reimagining the entire journey that many organisations find hard to achieve after years of incremental improvements. As such, it is not a tactical evolution of the current state. Finally specialists are taken from every function and charged with testing the reimagined journeys and processes from every angle.

Once a new customer experience has been designed, tested and refined, the next step is to develop the technology infrastructure to support it. Integrating new processes with legacy systems in a cost effective way is a challenge most organisations face in digitising their customer journeys. Then achieving customer adoption of digital customer journeys looms as the final challenge.

## Digital Strategy: Taking a Three Horizon Lens

The digital strategy should take a '3 horizon lens' approach focusing on:

1. The here and now
2. Emerging opportunities (e.g., the next 3 to 5 years)
3. The unknown future.

Typically most organisations focus on (1) and (2) and less so on (3). To that end, some organisations create a team to specifically focus solely on (3).

## Digital Strategies, Types of Businesses and Ecosystems

Hagel & Singer (1999) refer to three types of businesses:

1. Customer relationship (customer intimacy)
2. Product innovation/leadership
3. Infrastructure (build and manage platforms for high volume, repetitive tasks).

These types of businesses have different economic, competitive and cultural imperatives, and hence their digital strategies will vary significantly. Reference has been made earlier in Chapter 1 to Deloitte's (2014) concept of 'short fuse and big bang' digital disruption on various industries.

Greenberg, Hirt and Smit (2017) from McKinsey contend that businesses can be grouped into three categories, with ecosystems emerging as a powerful source of value creation:

1. Linear value chains comprising a series of value-adding steps with the goals of producing and selling products (e.g., automotive assembly)
2. Horizontal platforms that cut across value chains, with companies operating under this model owning hard assets and sophisticated architecture, typically built around value-adding software and technology stacks (e.g., Google, Amazon, Facebook)
3. Any-to-any ecosystems (e.g., Uber, Airbnb) with these companies operating at the centre of platforms, but being distinctly asset light.

## HRs' Role in Promoting Innovation

HRs' extended role in digital disruption is explored in Chapter 7 but specifically with respect to innovation, HR can influence and facilitate innovation, catalysing the organisation by contributing to:

- Creating an innovation context;
- Selecting innovation players, with a focus on convergence (i.e., bringing together people from various disciplines).

Creating an innovation context includes developing and encouraging the following characteristics and settings:

- Valuing flexibility, diversity, risk taking, and accelerated learning;
- Creating a physical and safe psychological environment that promotes collaboration, ideation and challenge;
- Embracing the reality that true innovation brings with it successes and failures, small wins and profound breakthroughs;

*Note.* *There is a need to reframe failure as not learning fast enough. Most work places are failure intolerant and so are not naturally conducive to risk taking and learning.*

- Openly recognising and rewarding both innovation efforts and outcomes;
- Promoting relentless learning as an organisational staple.

As external pressures have become more disruptive and complex, business models need to rely on more integrated, cross boundary approaches to solve harder problems. Selecting innovation players involves bringing the right people together, resulting in a collaborative effort as teams spark off each other. It goes without saying that it's vitally important to have leaders authentically supporting and actively driving innovation.

Chapter 3

# Three Other Current Trends Impacting on the Workplace & Workers

## 3.1 The Changing Nature of Work & Workers

Rapid change is not limited to technology, but also encompasses society and demographics. The changing nature of work, combined with the changing nature of the worker, is presenting new challenges for human resource management and global business strategy. Accordingly three other major trends (apart from technology) impacting upon organisations, the workplace and the worker include:

1. Longevity and the ageing workforce
2. Lower growth economy
3. Changing family structures.

These three trends are elaborated upon below.

## 3.2 Longevity & the Ageing Workforce

**The Significance of an Ageing Population**

> *A CIPD (2017) recent survey of 1,600 +55 year old workers indicated 37% believed that they would work beyond 65 years of age with the average age of retirement of 70 years.*

The workforce is becoming more age diverse, more ethnic diverse, more mobile and more autonomous. The number of older workers is on the rise. Approximately 30% of workers in the UK are over 50 years compared to 20% in the 1990s (CIPD, 2017).

The life expectancy for males and females continues to increase. Combined with lower birth rates, the median age of the population is increasing. The significance of this ageing population includes:

- A shift in the demand for products and services, with a growing cohort of older customers;

- The need for greater support for the health and wellbeing of an ageing workforce and population;
- The concept of retirement and pensions having to be re-examined because of their unaffordability, with people having to work longer and extend their careers, or develop new ones (see later in Chapter 4);
- The need for increased flexible work practices (see later in Chapter 4).

Not only are people working longer into traditional retirement years, but the vision of retirement and what it means to retire is evolving altogether. Career paths for mature workers include entrepreneurship, entering the gig economy, volunteerism, philanthropy, or joining a board of directors. These imminent retirees are looking to enrich the second phase of their life with substance and meaning.

## Caring Challenges of the 'Sandwich Generation'

The caring challenges of those caught in the 'Sandwich Generation' or intergenerational dependency (i.e., those who have dual caring responsibilities for children or teenagers and older parents), can be stressful. This Sandwich Generation are caught up managing the delicate balance between home and career.

It is estimated that approximately 45% of people 75 years and over will suffer from Alzheimer's disease (Alzeihemers.net, 2016) and will need some form of caring. For HR, the Sandwich Generation and their needs puts them squarely in the intersection where HR Strategy and Wellness come together. There is also a collateral emotional and engagement toll this places on the employees' colleagues, including management. Organisations will need to further assist in helping some of their employees (including the Sandwich Generation) to manage their work and caring responsibilities.

## Career Challenges

For more mature aged workers in particular, they will increasingly need to shape their own future, with existing barriers to the employment of older people (i.e., ageism prejudice). Many will need to generate income outside of the formal structures of government and the corporate world. Consequently there will be an increased focus on start-ups, self-employment, self-made work, and entrepreneurship—people will have to create their own job!

Notwithstanding, a more eclectic mix of how people work during their lifetime will develop according to their particular circumstances. Some will:

- Become more multi-skilled and multi-tasked as they move between diverse roles in different industries;
- React against working for larger corporations;
- Move in and out of 'getting a job and making a job', as the lines between traditional jobs and entrepreneurship become more blurred.

Adaptability, flexibility and relationship building will be requisite key soft skills. That said, more mature workers are likely to be less digitally savvy but nevertheless may be more flexible with respect to working hours and job types. Traditional career and job norms will no longer apply with people having to find their own pathway (refer to Appendix C on Careers in the Contemporary Workplace).

Edgar and Edgar (2017) contend that we have to look at the pattern of lifespan in different ways. An ageing workforce will experience continuous cycles of work, learning and leisure. The linear career development pathway cannot survive in the future of work. Work and longevity are positively correlated, with the prime years now considered to be 50 to 75 years, so retirement needs to be looked at differently.

## 3.3 Lower Growth Economy

Since the Global Financial Crisis in 2008, many of the world's economies, particularly in Europe and the US, have struggled to emerge from this recession, experiencing relatively low growth rates. China of course is contrary to this trend, but generally the outlook appears to be one of only moderate global growth. In advanced economies, there is weak demand with little evidence of the economy returning to the pre-recession level. The spread of global value chains seems to have reached its limit, even declined with a return to world trade's glory days appearing unlikely (Gittons, 2017). Rates of GDP are decreasing with stagnant labour forces. The new normal is slow growth while meeting the challenges from unseen competition with new business models from multiple and diverse markets.

# 3. Three Other Current Trends Impacting on the Workplace & Workers

*Note. Reference has been made in Chapter 4.2 relating to the growth of lower paid jobs-stagnant wages and increased protectionism.*

## 3.4 Changing Family Structures

Reference has been made above to more people falling into the 'Sandwich Generation'. Families are also having children later. Offspring are living at home longer prior to 'leaving the nest' due to housing unaffordability. Many families now rely on the income from dual career couples for their economic survival, with more females becoming the major breadwinner in the family.

*Note. Approximately 25% of people aged between 18 to 25 years live at home in Australia with this trend on the increase. They are known as KIPPERS (Kids In Parents Pockets Eroding Retirement Savings) (Salt, 2017). Factors instrumental in this trends include mobile phones replacing a single house hold land line, several television sets, the provision of additional space and privacy, and more relaxed attitudes of parents to overnight stays of partners.*

## 3.5 Other Recent Past Workplace & Workforce Developments

Other recent past workplace and workforce developments (i.e., over the past 20 or 30 years) leading up to digital disruption are summarised in Appendix A, including their impacts on organisations and individuals. These impacts should be read in conjunction with those included in Chapter 4

Chapter 4

# The Impact on Organisations, Jobs and People

## 4.1 The Impact on Organisations

Organisations face a radically shifting context for the workforce, the workplace, and the world of work. These shifts have changed the rules for nearly every organisational people practice, from learning, to management, to the definition of work itself. Organisations are now powered by accelerated connectivity, the trend of remote workers and increased consumer demands and needs. Today's digital workforce is more global and more automated than ever.

Business and HR leaders can no longer continue to operate according to old paradigms. They must now embrace new ways of thinking about their companies, their talent, and their role in global social issues. They must navigate through the fast-paced and unpredictable workplace environment where technology is transforming the workplace.

In summary, the multiple factors affecting how organisations manage their people include:

- Technology: internet, mobile devices, email instant messaging, collaboration tools and more are changing the traditional office environment with the workforce mantra of 'anyone, anywhere, anytime with any device;
- Multiple generations, cultures and locations: demographic shifts, geographic dispersion, a multi-cultural workforce composition and changing family structures all placing added pressure on how organisations engage their workforce;
- The contingent workforce: outsourcing and the extended or expanded workforce.

The new challenge is to establishing the right workforce at the right cost to execute the business strategy. Organisations must:

- Understand the demand their new business strategy and model will place on the future workforce;
- Understand how well their supply chain of people can meet the demand; and
- Then close the gap between their existing or legacy workforce, and supply and demand.

The key topics or themes of jobs, borderless working, flexible work practices, the extended workforce, careers and learning, organisational design, leadership, culture, people management practices and agility are examined in this Chapter.

# 4.2 The Impact on Jobs

**Technology: Both a Blessing and a Curse!**

Throughout history people have lost their jobs to machines. First the manual, then the clerical, and now it is feared the intellectual and conceptual due to technology. There has long been a relationship between technological change and productivity improvement. Work and work assignments are optimised by technology. For example, computers and email have long cut a swathe through business processes that once relied on pen and paper. Moving from the eras of industrialisation and services industries to the era of globalisation and technology has lead to significant changes in the nature of careers and employment development, with shorter tenures and more cyclical work. History shows that most workers tend to be highly resilient and adaptive.

The 4IR brings threats as well as opportunities, promising to revolutionise work, but potentially endangering the economic structures that have been built around the traditional notion of employment. There will be new freedoms to think, create, work remotely and travel more easily, but some people will be left behind in the white water turbulence (see below reference to some males and the mismatch of desired and available jobs). The 4IR is both a blessing and a curse: displacing jobs and mass redundancies, but improving the quality and longevity of people's lives!

The elimination of jobs through technology is predicted to be massive, but this has been predicted in the past since the early days of automation. Deloitte's modelling (Benedikt and Osborne, 2013) suggests that almost 5m Australian jobs (approximately 40% of the workforce) face a high probability of being replaced by computers in the next 10-15 years. This job loss is predicted to extend to service occupations, transportation, logistics, office and administrative support. Benedikt and Osborne predict 47% of today's jobs will be redefined within 20 years.

> *Note.* These predictions don't account for the generation of new digital jobs and new non-digital jobs (refer to Chapter 6, Steps 6 and 7 for further analysis and discussion

Others are more conservative in their future predictions. Sundararajan's (2017) and KRC's research findings suggest that the first wave of automation won't result in massive job displacement despite the media's fascination with the so-called 'Robot Apocalypse'. Automation will free up business leaders and employees to spend more time perfecting work projects and improving client relationships. The business case for technology is therefore not exclusively reliant on replacing jobs and people and saving money. It's also about enhancing human enabled business processes resulting in enhanced efficiency and task management.

For newly created jobs and some modified existing jobs, a greater emphasis will be placed on systems thinking, creativity, complex problem solving, collaboration and the fostering of deeper relationships. Computers are still relatively weak at:

- Social intelligence (interacting successfully with one another);
- Perception and manipulation; and
- Creative intelligence.

AI can learn fast and make accurate decisions but it cannot match the human wisdom of making contextual decisions. Technology has its limitations – it cannot inspire like humans!

## More About the Automation and Redefining of Jobs

Although consumers have largely gone digital, the digitisation of jobs, and of the tasks and activities within them, is still in the early stages, according to a recent study by Chui, Manyika, and Miremadi (2015) from the McKinsey Global Institute. Automation of jobs will result in disaggregating jobs into their component tasks and subtasks, and then hiving off those that can be automated. It will force organisations to figure out how to reassemble the remaining tasks into something that makes a new kind of sense, even as it reconceptualises the very idea of what a job is.

Once roles and tasks are broken down, the newly constructed jobs that result must be reaggregated into some greater whole, or 'box,' on the organisation chart. Those boxes then need a new relation to each other. For some organisations, this automation of jobs may prove powerfully liberating, making them far more agile, healthy, and high performing. For others, it may initiate a collapse into internal dysfunction as people try to figure out what their jobs are, who is doing what, and where and why.

> *Note. Disaggregation of jobs has been occurring for quite some time. For example in the HR domain, elements of HR have been broken down into various disciplines or specialities (compensation, recruitment, organisational development, etc.).*
> *Conversely aggregation of jobs has occurred in the last two decades, with the advent of*

*personal computers and the internet (email communication replacing facsimile and telex machines). Word processing and communications have been absorbed into most white and pink collar jobs, making the previous traditional roles of secretaries or personal assistants almost obsolete.*

Traditionally robots and computers have been harnessed to perform routine physical activities better and more economically than humans, but now they are increasingly capable of accomplishing activities that include cognitive capabilities. Every occupation includes multiple types of activity, each of which has different requirements for automation. McKinsey estimate that very few occupations (less than 5%) are candidates for full automation. However every occupation has partial automation potential. Those industries that are more susceptible to automation include: manufacturing, accommodation, food servicing and the retail trade. So while technology will continue to transform tasks within jobs, the occupation itself will remain and not disappear.

## New Cooperation Between Workers and Technology

While much of the current debate about automation has focused on the potential for mass unemployment, people will need to continue working alongside machines. Many workers will have to change, but new types of work will be created. Humans will still be needed in the workforce, but a new degree of cooperation will be required between workers and technology. This new type of work will involve an increased focus on planning and coordinating, supervising and decision-making.

As Tom Davenport and Julia Kirby (2016) emphasise in their book *Only Humans Need Apply*, this requires recognising that 'augmentation means starting with what minds and machines do individually today and figuring how that work could be deepened rather than diminished by a collaboration between the two.' For example, jobs in manufacturing and agriculture have transformed from high touch to high tech.

## Some of the Benefits of Automation

The current wave of automation not only changes jobs, but the entire work process, whether in services, research, and development, sourcing, production or distribution. In short connectivity trumps hierarchies. Automation can deliver a variety of business benefits, apart from labour substitution cost reductions, including:

- Getting closer to the customer (e.g., web cams, analysing responses to email campaigns with click through rates);
- Improved performance/productivity gains and higher safety (e.g., oil and gas operations);
- Improved industrial operations (e.g., reducing maintenance costs in mining operations);
- Optimisation of knowledge work (e.g., performing rules-based tasks);
- Harnessing the power of nature (e.g., crop management in agriculture);
- Increasing scale and speed (e.g., analysing models).

Automation coupled with increased protectionism/anti globalisation, may result in a return of some jobs back to homeland that had previously been outsourced overseas.

## Jobs 'At Risk' and 'Safe' Jobs

The degree of change of jobs being disrupted by technology will be based on whether roles are primarily manual or cognitive, and comprised of routine or non-routine tasks (Microsoft 2018)

|  | Routine | Non-routine |
|---|---|---|
| Cognitive | More likely to be automated due to recent advancements in AI and data analytics. Example professions:<br>• Office assistant<br>• Sales agent<br>• X-ray technician<br>• Paralegal | Less likely to be automated by AI due to nature of task and need for 'human' touch. Example professions:<br>• Managers<br>• Engineers<br>• Healthcare workers<br>• Creative<br>• Researchers |
| Manual | Likely to be automated by robots, 3D printing, IoT and other advances. Example professions:<br>• Assembly line workers<br>• Mechanic | Lack of uniform need but may still be automated due to advances in AI, IoT and other technologies. Example professions:<br>• Hospitality worker<br>• Security guard<br>• Maintenance worker<br>• Hairdresser |

As indicated in the above table, some low skilled, routine or manual tasks, requiring minimal creative intelligence, and easily replicable by machine, are at risk from automation. Other low skilled jobs requiring little education are likely to be difficult to automate (e.g., cleaning, food preparation).

> *Note. Automation of some jobs raises ethical, legal and safety issues in the event of mistakes being made and possible harm to property and/or persons.*

Moderately skilled jobs, requiring some education and training, represent the largest demographic in the workforce and also the ones most at risk of extinction. The routine element of these jobs that are predictable and repetitive in industries such as manufacturing, administration, and transportation, lead them to automation (i.e., transaction based jobs).

Jobs that require complex movement, creativity, non-routine, are socially focused and involve managing others are relatively safe from automation (i.e., interaction or new world jobs). These include nursing, teaching, the arts, physiotherapy, etc., that are more the domain of female workers.

Thus some jobs will be eliminated, many jobs will be transformed or look different, and new jobs will be created. Overall, the jobs of the future are likely to be better, safer, more stimulating, and more socially impactful.

## Some New Jobs are Different to Old Jobs

While the engine of job creation is still running, it has shifted into a lower gear, creating more lower middle-class jobs with more stagnant incomes where supply is relatively plentiful. Some of these jobs are non-full time (i.e., permanent part-time), that may suit some, whilst for others, may constitute under employment. The rate of human displacement is most probably faster than the rate of job creation.

> *Note. Supply and demand governs wages. Highly regulated labour markets protect supply including licensing of skilled, semi-skilled jobs and professionals (e.g., doctors). Unionised jobs also protect supply.*

The new jobs that are being created are different to the jobs that are disappearing with a mismatch between desired and available jobs. For example, some traditional male occupations are drying up (e.g., manufacturing) being replaced by lower paid roles in the service and health industries. As a consequence, some males are finding it increasingly difficult to adjust to the limited employment opportunities, and their suitability to these new job characteristics. They are experiencing an identity and skills crisis.

Hence there are social change implications as well as technical change implications for those displaced workers experiencing difficulties re-entering the workforce. Yet when men, especially white men, enter female-dominated fields, they are paid more and promoted faster than women—a phenomenon known as 'the glass escalator'.

## The Future Workforce

There will be a need to build new pools of skilled digital employees to move into expanding niches of the economy. According to Deloitte Access Economics (2017 Australia's Digital Pulse report), technology is likely to generate increased demand for two types of workers:

1. Specialist ICT workers – to develop, operate and maintain ICT systems with approximately half directly employed in ICT-related industries such as computer system design, telecommunications services and internet service provision. The other half are employed elsewhere in areas such as professional services, public administration and finance.
2. The broader workforce using ICT – includes those who use ICT regularly even if it's not the primary focus of their jobs, including a wide variety of occupations such as accountants, legal professionals, office managers, architects, and engineers. About 90% of jobs today require basic digital skills such as sending emails, searching the internet, using a word processor. Workers need to be able to manage their digital identities and have a basic knowledge of cybersecurity. This is a prerequisite to gaining more specialist skills and transitioning into roles where technology platforms are essential.

## Digital Skills in Demand

As described above it's important to differentiate between digital skills for the general workforce and the greater degree of specialisation for ICT professionals. ICT skills that will be in demand include:

- Data interpreters – data analysts and scientist top the list of professionals that employers will rely on to interpret the torrent of information produced by digital technologies. Specialists in areas such as mathematics and statistics will be in strong demand as industries apply big data analytics, visualization and other tools.
- Software and app developers – very high growth likely in these roles that involve developing new mobile applications and software solutions in specific areas.
- Technology system supervisors – additional demand for workers who can manage technology systems as well as provide quality assurance (e.g., sensor deployment and maintenance workers, robotic fault diagnostics personnel, 3D printer technicians, drone delivery schedulers, autonomous fleet managers).
- Digital experience designers – design new visualisation systems that allow people to take advantage of augmented and virtual reality that will be required in a range of industries including retail, tourism, healthcare, and education and training. Skilled experts will also create intuitive interfaces for apps, devices and machines, including digitally enabled household appliances and cars. Professionals in this area are often referred to a user experience (UX) and user interface (UI) experts.
- Change managers – ongoing demand for managers with digital and business skills to steer organisations through change including platform upgrades and business process redesigns, adoption of cloud technologies, mobile devices and augmented reality interfaces.
- Technology sales and marketing professionals – skilled in commercializing and explaining new digital products and services.
- Professional advisers – need for new professional advisory services.

As technology is integrated into business processes, there will be an additional demand for regulatory, legal, policy and compliance expertise in areas such as personal privacy, security, and identity management need.

## The Challenge of Upskilling

Automation will continue to define the tasks we do in the future. Organisations will face a greater demand for highly skilled workers as job requirements change. Friedman (2016) has coined the term 'stempathy' describing the highest paying jobs for the future being those that incorporate the following skills: science, technology, engineering and maths, combined with empathy for people.

The greatest challenge will be to upskill current employees for the ever-changing world of work, and to increase the relevance and resilience of people. Their employability will depend not only on what they know, but also on their ability to learn new skills. HR can support digital transformation by expanding digital literacy, giving employees access to digital skills tools, and training with courses (preferably in digital format) on topics like data science, business intelligence, digital design, marketing and virtual collaboration. Additionally for those seeking to change career paths, training in handling career transitions will assist in their redeployment.

## 4.3 Borderless Working

### Older Ways of Working Becoming Less Effective

Changing customer and employee needs and behaviours, combined with global technology changes (e.g., the cloud, social and collaborative technologies), in addition to the emergence of new business models, make older ways of working and delivering products and services far less effective. A more mobile and fluid workforce is being created that is demanding new ways of doing their jobs. The workforce is moving towards a hybrid way of working with office, home and mobile work places becoming equally important.

The workplace of the future will have multiple definitions and manifestations with new opportunities presenting to work in different ways, and to combine work, family and personal life. The barriers and divide between work and life have almost disappeared. We are witnessing the rise of the 'pyjama workforce' where the 9 to 5 commute no longer exists.

Thus 'borderless working' with the mantra of working with 'anyone, anywhere, at anytime from any device' has now become the new norm. Work happens wherever you are! Managing in a borderless workplace is about orchestrating people and resources, rather than establishing control and command. Trust becomes a more important intangible commodity in this new workplace given that workers need to self-regulate, operating within a culture of autonomy, accountability and results. Telecommuting (the umbrella term used to describe any work occurring outside of the traditional office) comes in many flavours. Notwithstanding, most companies want workers at the office or equivalent, at least some if not most of the time.

## The New Office Environment

Businesses are finding new ways to organise their offices. The desire for flexibility, the reality of employee mobility, and the pursuit of lower real estate costs will push the office of 2020 towards more multi-use facilities and arrangements that become just one of many places employees work. Offices should be looked at as a destination with amenities, and creating an environment that attract workers.

Workplaces should be designed to align with the needs of teams and individuals catering for collaborative ideation, interactive problem solving, virtual participation, or focused immersion. Common characteristics of an open office design include large desks, informal lounges and gardens. Open office design encourages better collaboration and interaction among employees as opposed to the isolated cubicles of the past. Spaces and patterns of work should be designed to accommodate the natural biorhythms and work style preferences of individuals to optimise wellbeing, creativity and productivity. This palette of places design includes standing table open spaces for quick meetings, couch rooms for more relaxed catch ups, and isolated spaces for deeper work. The idea is to cater to the different tasks office workers need to do throughout the day which a mere stationary desk arrangement simply can't do. This flexibility gives workers the power to choose their working conditions. Unified wired and wireless network infrastructure is emerging as the new normal in network infrastructure. The office has become a place for collaboration whereas home is a place for concentration.

That said, the results of initiatives like activity based work, 'hot desking' and encouraging people to work from home have been mixed. Some have found it difficult to adjust to continually working at a different desk plus the noise factor in a more open office setting. Some employees have taken advantage of the working from home perk using this flexibility to attend to non-work matters and their personal life. Trust is therefore an issue for some organisations and managers with respect to those working from home.

*Note. Contract arrangements should be put in place for those working from home.*

Furthermore, there are pros and cons for flexible work in the modern workplace. Some people find it difficult to switch off or feel anxious, with others feeling under surveillance. Yet others feel empowered by having remote access, helping them to work more flexibly and productively. Remote working also opens up the jobs market to those who may not previously have had access.

## 4.4 Flexible Work Practices

### Increased Use of Flexible Work Practices

Borderless working, demographics and changes in employee preferences will reinforce the shift to more flexible work practices. Many markets have aging labour pools that will drive more flexible work as retirees opt for contractor and part-time roles. The increased use of flexible work practices will result in a more dispersed workforce with connectivity becoming even more important. Society is becoming more tied to its mobile devices in the attention economy. Cloud computing obviates an organisation's need to rely exclusively on internal resources, making available a variety of IT services online. The benefits of the cloud in the workplace are elaborated upon later in Chapter 8.

### Two Types of Flexible Work Practices

Flexible work practices can be categorised according to two types:

- Mandatory (employer oriented); and
- Voluntary (worker oriented).

The flexible work practices that employers have introduced over the past two decades or so to cut or minimise labour costs, has now 'come back to bite'. Overall people are demanding more flexibility and lifetime choices. Coupled with technological advancements (i.e., access to the web, emails, etc.), they are now demanding the flexibility to work when and where they want, particularly with the inefficiencies of longer commuting times. Furthermore people tend to work in bursts and lulls anyway, according to different biorhythms. Some are 'morning people' and some are 'evening people', so this flexibility in working patterns may potentially result in increased productivity and work quality.

> *Note. The emphasis for employees/workers should be less about work-life balance and more about work-life integration. The term 'work-life balance' implies that work isn't part of life! It implies an exclusivity and inherent conflict between work and other life domains that is not necessarily the case.*

## The Rise of the 'Gig' Economy

> *Wikipedia defines Gig as 'slang for a live musical performance.' Originally coined in the 1920s by jazz musicians, the term, short for the word 'engagement', now refers to any aspect of performing such as assisting with performance and attending a musical performance. More broadly, the term 'gigging' means having paid work, being employed. A gig economy is an environment in which temporary positions are common and organisations contract with independent workers for short-term engagements.*

The 'gig' economy has been trending the last few years partly as a result of crowdsourcing platforms. The gig economy is part of a shifting cultural and business environment that also includes the sharing economy, the gift economy and the barter economy. The rise of this economy has suited some people whereas for others, it has resulted in their underemployment.

In a gig economy, businesses save resources in terms of benefits, office space and training. They also have the ability to contract with experts for specific projects who might be too high-priced to maintain on staff. From the perspective of the freelancer, a gig economy can improve work-life balance over what is possible in most jobs. Ideally, the model is powered by independent workers selecting jobs that they're interested in, rather than them being forced into a position where, unable to attain employment, they pick up whatever temporary gigs they can land. The disadvantages of the gig economy for these latter people include little if any job security, intermittent and unpredictable schedules, low pay, and minimal benefits, with little safe guards in place.

According to McCrindle (2017) in a survey of approximately 1,000 casual or contract workers in Australia, 57% chose to work this way with 63% of Baby Boomers the most likely to choose this mode of working, more-so than Gen Y (50%) and Gen X (52%). Work-life balance was a key driver of their choice, with those having control over their work-life balance indicating a satisfaction rate of 90% compared to those without such choice indicating a satisfaction rate of 26%. The top three industry sectors employing casual workers were:

1. Education and training
2. Health care, community care and social assistance
3. Retail trade.

> **Note**. *An alternative term for this new disruptive economy where people work when, where and how they want is 'HIP'. This is an acronym for 'Highly Interconnected & Productive' workers and workplaces.*

## 'Workation'

> *Workation definition: A paid work trip that can be combined with aspects of taking a vacation. From 'work' + 'vacation'.*

Reference has been made earlier to the distinction between professional and personal life having become increasingly blurred. We now have the advent of 'Workation' where people are on vacation, but nevertheless reading their emails and periodically attending to some work related matters. With today's fast paced business environment, it is becoming increasingly difficult for some people to be completely cut off from work related matters. That said, organisations have an obligation to assist their employees balance personal and professional life/work demands.

## 4.5 Growth of the Extended Workforce & Talent Management Strategies

### The Multi-Modal Workforce

Traditional employment paradigms are being challenged by technology. The future workforce will continue to shift to a more multi-modal one with a mix of permanents, contractors and freelancers (i.e., the 'casualisation' of the workforce). The trend towards open talent networks (OTN) and a variable labour cost model with independent work is growing at an accelerated pace. Technology devices and platforms have created the infrastructure to source and deliver freelance work.

This surging trend towards redefining work is being driven in part by the desire by some to work remotely as an independent professional. McKinsey (2017) estimate that between 20–30% of the working age population in the US and the European Union is engaged in independent work, with 70% choosing this type of work. The remaining 30% are reported to be turning to it out of necessity because they cannot find a job that meets their needs. The % of independent work that is conducted on digital platforms is 15%, but is growing rapidly with technology based jobs dominating the freelance sector.

The advantages of independent work for organisations are:

- Lower cost structures;
- Faster response times;
- Better quality work with the use of specialists.

However the downside of more project based independent work for individuals is job insecurity, and the associated wellbeing and stress concerns.

## A Unified Talent Management Strategy

Contingent workers have been previously viewed as second-rate citizens in most organisations. Relabelling workers as 'talent' has elevated their importance from being viewed as a costly unit of labour to that of strategic human capital. Mindsets are also now shifting from one of an ownership economy to a sharing economy. Talent portfolio management integrates the contingent talent to align the capabilities and development of the workforce, resulting in a unified talent management strategy comprising permanents, contractors and freelancers.

*Note.* Contingent work is defined as part-time, temporary, or contracted.

Employers will more regularly tap into non-traditional sources of employees, including those who have received additional degrees or specialised online training. This extended workforce, part of whom is highly mobile and dynamic, is now increasingly being viewed as a strategic asset for high value/knowledge roles. Organisations will rely more on networks of temporary contributors from outside of the organisation. The expertise that can be captured by full-time employment is a microcosm of the total expertise available.

Applications of this extended workforce, include:

- A new supply chain of talent;
- Supplementing existing core employees;
- Importation of expertise;
- Project work;
- Solving specific problems.

### The Challenge of Managing Many Different 'Deals'

People management is becoming more complex with this increase in outsourcing and the growth of the extended workforce. There is a requirement to structure and manage many different employment relationships and contractual 'deals' (i.e., psychological contracts), whilst at the same time maintaining a level of consistency or uniformity.

### The Impact of Investments in Talent Development Versus Organisational Development

It should be noted that according to Ulrich's (2017) research, investments in organisational development initiatives (e.g., strategic workforce planning) have four times more impact than investments in talent development. The analogy is that in the case of sporting teams, the best players normally play in the winning team. Teams win championships and not individuals. In other words, the team effort and performance matters more than and surpasses individual's efforts and performance.

## 4.6 Careers

By way of background, career models/types in the contemporary workplace have been elaborated upon in Appendix C, including the career implications for both organisations and individuals. Apart from digital disruption and its implications for career groups, three other career themes are now further emerging include: (1) portfolio careers, (2) hybrid workers, and (3) longer careers.

## Digital Disruption and Career Groups

As referred to earlier, the convergence of digital technologies is creating new roles, augmenting existing ones and rendering others redundant. The workforce can be divided into four career groups:

1. Career starters – young people starting off and learning skills.
2. Shifters – workers in industries already in decline or facing significant disruption where most tasks and processes may be automated (e.g., automotive and manufacturing sectors). These workers will need to embark on new careers that require digital skills and training and enhance their capabilities in non-routine tasks.
3. Reinventors – workers in primarily processed roles where current skills may not be required because a significant proportion of the process may be automated. They may need to reinvent their roles and upskill to higher value jobs (e.g., accountants, legal clerks, logistics workers).
4. Perennials – less likely to see their work changed substantially by technology, primarily in interpersonal-roles, or jobs unlikely to be automated. Technology will augment these worker's roles (e.g., engineers, educators and researchers, creative and artists, project managers)

## The Growth of More Flexible Portfolio Careers

As organisations grow flatter and more matrixed, traditional full-time employees will have opportunities for 'portfolio careers' that involve more frequent switching of roles (i.e., talent mobility). To do that, employees will need to take greater ownership of their mid-career learning and development activities. More employees will need cross-functional skills to support new digital ways of doing business.

For example, employees will find themselves working across functional lines to create and deliver new digital product bundles, or to interact with customers through new channels. All functions including HR, Legal, Finance, Operations, Marketing, will seek out analytical capabilities and technical skills. Because these skills will be in short supply, organisations will need to reduce the rigid boundaries that separate functions to enable more hybrid roles. As mentioned earlier, there is also a new focus on convergence—

bringing together disciplines such as sales, marketing, design, finance, and IT onto cross-functional teams to build products and solutions faster.

## Hybrid and Chameleon Workers

The impact to the workforce of technology change is massive—a game changer to any traditional notion of workforce that we've come to know. Technology is transforming the skill set demands with a requirement for more flexible, multi-skilled employees with technical proficiency and the ability to adapt quickly to change. Businesses will need hybrid workers who not only understand their own sector, but complex digital technology as well.

Saxena (2016) refers to 'chameleon workers'—those that are able to adapt quickly to change, learn new skills in a short space of time, and move seamlessly from assignment to assignment. More so than ever before, organisations will need to engage, motivate, retain, and attract talent to support the continued survivability of the company. Employees will pursue more flexible roles and varied employment models and career paths. Communication and problem solving skills will become increasingly more important core skills. As networks and ecosystems replace organisational hierarchies, the traditional question: *For who do you work* has been replaced by: *With whom do you work?*

## Longer Careers and Skill Requirements

Employees now enjoy the prospect of up to 60-year careers. Yet at the same time, the half-life of skills is rapidly falling. To keep pace with these changes, Chief Learning Officers (CLOs) must now become the catalysts for a focus on continuous career development and next-generation careers, while also thinking about how to support the overall growth of the business. CLOs should become part of the entire employee experience, delivering learning solutions that inspire people to reinvent themselves, develop deep skills, and contribute to the learning of others.

The goal is a learning environment adapted to a world of increased employee mobility. As referred to above, interdisciplinary skills development is critical because these capabilities align with the organisational shift to networks of teams. Learning should encourage, and even push, people to move across jobs. Problem solving, creativity, project management, emotional intelligence, communication, listening, and moral and ethical decision-making are all essentially human skills that every organisation needs—now and in the future. The future workforce will require a balance of these soft skills and technical skills.

## 4.7 Learning

### The Increased Importance of Learning

We live in the age of 'Digital Darwinism', a term first coined in 1999 by Evan I Schwartz who defined it as 'an era where technology and society are evolving faster than businesses can naturally adapt.' Today's organisations are suffering from a severe case of structural lag, where their internal time clocks are increasingly out of pace with the external pace of change (Pillans, 2017). In this era of unprecedented change, complexity and uncertainty, the need to learn fast, adapt and manage change has never been greater for organisational survival. Learning must move from the periphery to the centre of organisational growth and change. There is a need to rethink how the workforce is developed—everything from learning methods used, the content delivered, and the technology used to deliver it.

### Shifts in Learning and Training Delivery

> *Learning is moving from an organisational centric push approach to a learner centric pull approach… Collaborative digital platforms, where learners share their experiences, and develop new skills and ideas together, are bringing learning right to the heart of the workplace (Williamson, cited in Pillans, 2017).*

The new digital landscape has turned L&D strategies on their heads putting a new lens on learning. Learning delivery is shifting away from a traditional class room setting and moving online courtesy of new technology, making learning resources available wherever and whenever needed, putting employees in the drivers seat of their own learning agenda, enabling them to take control of their learning including what, how and where (refer later to the section on digital learning strategies). That said, there is the danger of losing focus and control over learning as alluded to in the following section on the alignment between strategy and learning.

Organisations are shifting away from designing and delivering bespoke content towards 'curating' best-in-class content from a variety of different internal and external sources. Lengthy internal courses and time consuming presentations are being replaced with technology enabled on demand smaller chunks of information with the right information being provided in the right way in the right time. This helps to solve the problem of people remembering only a small proportion of what they learn in the class room. Training is moving more into performance support systems that provide the information people need to complete a task when it arises.

Furthermore learning is being democratised—where it is much more widely available, getting rid of the barriers in terms of cost, location, time language. Social learning—learning from others—is becoming an increasingly important element of learning strategy with organisations investing in technology to support it. The market for learning platforms has exploded in recent years. Organisations are using dialogue and discussion as the basis for learning through co-creation, often through experiential learning or action learning.

With regard to education and qualifications, there are the challenges of full-time study and the nascent concept within the tertiary education system that remains structured around courses with multiple modules completed in specific time frames. New models of learning should be adopted with the elevation of micro credentials (low cost and flexible) and alternative qualifications. These options are increasingly being recognized as legitimate alternative qualifications and education pathways.

## Defining the Organisation

Ultimately an organisation is about its critical capability(s) and competencies that deliver value in the form of products and services (i.e., what the organisation is good at). These capabilities and competencies are a product of the collective skills, abilities and expertise of an organisation. They are the outcome of investments in staffing, training, compensation, communication, systems, structures, and resources - they represent the way that people and resources are brought together to accomplish work. They form the identity and personality of the organisation by defining what it is good at doing and what it is. They are the source of an organisation's competitive advantage and its sustainability. The business strategy should focus on maintaining and strengthening these critical capability(s) and core competencies.

*Note. A capability may be viewed or defined as the sum of expertise and capacity.*

## Where to Start with Your Learning Strategy?

Therefore the place to start in determining an organisation's learning strategy is to ask:

- What are the critical capability(s) and core competencies of the organisation?
- What is the strategic intent of the organisation?
- How does it realise that intent through people and the organisation?

Every organisation or firm operates in a unique competitive situation. To implement its strategy and achieve its goals, each firm must develop and build capabilities and competencies that are critical to its strategic intent. The learning strategy should reflect this development taking into account current and future business priorities. Unless an organisation has the capabilities that it needs, it will be unable to execute its strategy effectively.

Learning should therefore focus on developing the critical or differentiating capabilities and core competencies needed to execute the business strategy. These capabilities and competencies are a product of the collective skills, abilities and expertise of an organisation. They are the outcome of investments in staffing, training, compensation, communication, systems, structures, and resources - they represent the way that people and resources are brought together to accomplish work. They form the identity and personality of the organisation by defining what it is good at doing and what it is.

Investments in learning should be clearly defined and targeted in areas that enhance the organisation's competitive advantage. For example, a strategy of product innovation might lead to an investment in learning of design thinking, whereas a cost management strategy would mean investing in lean management skills.

*Note. Design thinking (also known as human-centered design) is an approach to problem solving and solution generation that puts the user at the centre, and uses such tactics as empathy, rapid ideation, low fidelity prototyping and testing to develop and implement ideas that create impact.*

One of the top priorities for Learning professionals is developing future leaders. While it is necessary and valuable to do this, as Pillans (2017) rightly points out, the learning function risks being fixated on esoteric issues such as 'leadership' or 'talent' at the expense of the critical task of investing in key capabilities for growth, such as selling, commercial and digital skills.

## Establishing a Learning Governance

The establishment of a Learning Council or similar governance body enables formal input from the business about learning plans. Such governance structures and communication lines enable a dialogue between key business stakeholders and learning leaders. These structures also impose rigour and discipline around learning, including defining associated evaluation measures to determine whether the outcomes are being delivered.

## Two Types of Learning

*Pillans (2017) Categorises Two Types of Learning*

1. Productive learning where there is a focus on the goal of improving for example productivity or quality or customer service. It is about conveying information about tasks that is already known, necessary for optimum performance, but is insufficient to ensure long standing organisational sustainability. Productive learning can bring everyone up to the standard of the current best performance, and serves largely to maintain the *status quo*.

2. Generative learning (or adaptive learning) involves creative problem solving, and is essentially a collaborative endeavour such as action learning and experiential learning that are based on co-creation. It focuses on growth and innovation and involves not only absorbing existing information, but also creating new solutions to unanticipated problems.

## Learnability and Learning Agility (Adaptive Learning)

*Learnability: The desire and ability to learn new skills for long-term employability. Learning agility: An individual's ability to continually acquire new skills, learn from experience, face new challenges, and perform well under changing conditions. It is the ability to apply knowledge, experience and expertise to new, unfamiliar situations.*

Learning is a two way street consisting of:

1. What the organisation may provide (including the channels and content)
2. The capacity of employees to learn—both their motivation (learnability) and capability (learning agility).

---

### Five Factors of Learning Agility

According to Swisher and Dai (2014), learning agility encompasses five factors:

1. Mental agility: ability to examine problems in unique and unusual ways
2. People agility: skilled communicator who can work with diverse people
3. Change agility: likes to experiment and comfortable with change
4. Results agility: delivers results in challenging, first time situations
5. Self-awareness: extent to which an individual knows their true strengths and weaknesses.

Learning agility can become a key organisational capability when applied to a critical mass of employees. It is an indication of the readiness of the workforce to adapt to or digest digital transformation. Refer to Chapter 6, Step 8.

## Digital Learning Strategies

Organisations need to formalise digital learning strategies to improve employee engagement and business outcomes. This is the foundation of a digital workplace. As referred to above, digital makes it possible to provide more targeted and flexible approaches to training by reducing worker's attendance of duplicate or unnecessary sessions.

Organisations should be focused on creating access to digital learning technology, providing business context and leadership insights, and a culture that supports learning. On-demand access to information is key, with many employees increasingly turning to their smartphones to find just-in-time answers to queries. As such, immediate needs and individuals' interests are increasingly directing peoples' learning using online searches to learn. L & D programs should allow for some self-direction. Employees have come to expect choice and are probably the best judges of what they need to learn.

Flipped classrooms are the disruptor of corporate learning with the following advantages:

- The cost of paying employees for their training time and travel is reduced;
- They are a highly self-organised learning format that sets the class room at the employees' preferred places;
- The virtual and on-line learning can be tackled during downtime at work or even home.

Furthermore mature learning organisations are increasingly discarding some of the long-held or traditional beliefs about how learning should be created and facilitated, and instead focusing on creating the right conditions, context and culture for learning to take place. This involves less focus on courses, curricula, and curation, and more on infrastructure, feedback loops, and collecting data to help employees make better decisions about their work and their own development.

## Digital Literacy/Intelligence

*Deakin University's Graduate Learning Outcome 3 (DU GLO 3) (2017) defines digital literacy as: Using technologies to find, use and disseminate information.*

*Wikipedia's definition of digital literacy is as follows: A digitally literate person will possess a range of digital skills, knowledge of the basic principles of computing devices, skills in using computer networks, an ability to engage in online communities and social networks while adhering to behavioural protocols, be able to find, capture and evaluate information, an understanding of the societal issues raised by digital technologies (such as big data), and possess critical thinking skills.*

*Catlin, Scanlan, and Willmont (2015) from McKinsey refer to the concept of a digital quotient defining it as follows: An understanding the strategic power of information technology, and having the ability to execute digital strategies for competitive business advantage.*

**Note.** *The terms 'digital literacy', 'digital quotient' and 'digital intelligence' have similar meanings and tend to be used interchangeably by various Subject Matter Experts.*

Digital literacy is the commercial acumen of the 21$^{st}$ century and the cornerstone of training in the 21$^{st}$ century workplace. It is an essential skill for effective participation in today's fast-paced digital world, with businesses relying on digital technology for all aspects of their operations. However measuring workforce digital literacy is an elusive goal. It's not practical to create a single measure for assessing the digital literacy of all workers at all levels in functional areas. Digital literacy training must be tailored to the needs and functions of the business, with help desk and other assistance, instruction and training resources provided as required. Thus organisations will need to invest more in the training of their staff in digital literacy, including cybersecurity.

**Note.** *One possibility for the future is for individuals to compile a Digital Education Passport that tracks their digital training activities (some of which may be just-in-time) and experience.*

Furthermore, gaining digital intelligence capabilities is not just a matter of procuring solutions and deploying them. The challenges to becoming a data-driven organisation are broad-based and require a multifaceted approach involving technology, new sources of data, new skills, and above all, leadership that not only supports but drives the entire organisation to adopt a dynamic data- driven culture (refer to Leadership later in this Chapter).

## 4.8 Organisational Design

**About Organisational Design**

*Organisational design involves the integration of structure, tasks, processes, responsibility and authority, and people to support or match the mission and business strategy.*

As referred to in the previous section, ultimately an organisation is about capabilities and competencies that deliver value in the form of products and services (i.e., what the organisation is good at). Organisational design deals with the structure and processes of the organisation, allowing it to achieve the purposes for which it was created. It should reflect the strategic intent of the organisation and incorporates four key issues:

1. Setting up the interface between the organisation and the customer group
2. Configuring resources to get the best value creating process
3. Integrating and supporting the various parts of the organisation to create synergy
4. Allocating resources to support the maintenance and strengthening of critical capabilities and core competencies that are the source of an organisation's competitive advantage and sustainability.

4. The Impact on Organisations, Jobs and People

## Recent Shifts in Organisational Design

The structure of organisations is under attack with digital transformation and the changing nature of work. Major restructuring of organisation charts, changes to roles and responsibilities, and re-engineered processes will be required in the drive for the adaptive organisation. Clearly there are and will be significant impacts on people and their jobs, with associated change management requirements to address these impacts.

It is important for organisations to become more nimble and responsive to change. Agility plays a central role in the organisation of the future, as companies race to replace structural hierarchies with networks of teams empowered to take action. It represents the ability to make timely, effective and sustained changes when and where those confer a performance advantage.

In many cases, apart from totally reworking organisational structures, digital transformation can be as much about collaborative methods. An organisation minus hierarchy equals collaboration, which is the new template and model of work.

Organisational design therefore needs to be aligned with the new world of work. It is progressively changing with hierarchies slimmed down or flattened, and further leveraging contingent and contract labour. These changes reflect the connection of internal silos, automation of key processes, and prioritising of core competencies, taking into account sophisticated supply chains and the need for connectivity. Some firms are reorganising around the customer life cycle with a customer centric organisational model.

The concept of matrix accountability is unavoidable as services span multiple organisational structures. These services and their supporting processes can be understood as horizontal management structures established and managed on top of traditional vertical silos. The matrix model accommodates functional specialization and end-to-end service lifecycle management. It manages and maintains core functions and allows resource flexibility and optimizes span of control to maximize one team behavior.

This shift in organisational forms away from functional boundaries and hierarchies in favour of fast-changing matrices may be complex with many horizontal interdependencies. People may sit on a number of teams at the same time. These teams may be static or deliberatively evolve. As noted earlier, they will pursue more flexible roles and varied employment models and career paths.

*Note. When silos characterise the organisation, responses to rapidly evolving customer needs are often too narrow, with key signals missed or acted upon too slowly. They also*

> *can breed a narrow parochial mentality of workers who hesitate to share information or collaborate across functions and department, all of which can be corrosive to culture. The interdisciplinary requirement of digital is at odds with this silo mentality.*

Another shift in organisational design is the establishment of Centres of Excellence. These Centres facilitate the building of new capabilities that can be deployed across both functional and new service teams. This enables flexibility and focus to create, develop, embed and transition to business as usual.

## The Challenges of Going Flat!

Hierarchically layered organisation can create the following difficulties: too many layers, inefficient decision-making, passing the buck, silo mentality, careerism, to name a few. The benefits of a flatter organisational hierarchy include:

- Creating a more agile business where people are freer to make decisions swiftly and are not weighed down by traditional bureaucracy;
- Empowering employees who are able to make decisions, make more meaningful contributions and are likely to be more engaged as a consequence;
- Reducing costs with lower overheads and management staff salaries.

Notwithstanding, going flat is not without its challenges. Amongst other things, it requires employees to be more capable and self-regulating, some adopting broader roles and implies a greater level of trust by management and employees. These challenges have been summarised in the five key areas below.

### 1. Leadership and Power

The goal of many of these flatter structures appears to be to establish a democratic culture where teams work together in harmony towards a shared vision. Often situational leaders emerge as a result of a flatter hierarchy. This may result in negative behaviour because power has been dispersed to a party that is not responsible for the outcome. Power should reside with the individual or team that is responsible and this dispersion must be explicit, if not by the organisation chart, then by other means. Without a title and power, most people feel no obligation to lead when things get tough.

Flat hierarchies require leaders to:

- Be skilled communicators, adept at prioritising and disseminating information;
- Understand their team and interact with them as peers, while still maintaining power;
- Be dynamic, able to make decisions rapidly based on consistent logic;
- Be aware of and knowledgeable about the context of their actions, including the legal implications;
- Lead with purpose and charisma, given that people now have more choice in who they may follow.

Furthermore, employees must be capable, self-sufficient and flexible where higher levels of trust prevail given that there is less management scrutiny of their activities.

## 2. Communication Channels

Without clear structure around roles and reporting lines, communications can become confused. There is a danger of poor decisions being made because necessary information hasn't been distributed or some people feeling left out because of poor or confused lines of communication. Leaders must take charge of communications and the prioritisation of information.

## 3. Matching a Skill Set to a Task

In flatter hierarchies, there tends to be much greater differences in the proficiency between individuals who appear similar based on their job titles. This can be misleading in terms of task allocation. Leaders must be able to identify the best mix of people resources to deliver tasks to the required quality and cost. To do this they need a clear skills inventory of the people in the organisation.

## 4. The Legal Context

The legislative environment has not kept pace with changes in this domain. Legally the law holds certain individuals more responsible than others for certain conduct of the organisation, whether they directly participate or not. A flat hierarchy does not excuse those individuals from their obligations. Organisations and leaders need to fully understand these obligations, and that the individuals so concerned are taking ownership and have the necessary authority to exercise that ownership.

### 5. *Roles Versus Responsibilities*

There is still a need for individuals and teams to be held responsible and accountable for outcomes (i.e., role clarity). Leaders need to hold people to account for their performance, to delegate responsibility fairly, and to set the tone for the behaviour that is acceptable within the organisation. A consensus seems to be forming that going flat can be effective, but removing too much structure is dangerous.

## Three Approaches to Organisational Design and Configuration

Three approaches to organisational design and configuration are presented below:

1. Mintzberg's Five Organisational Types/Configurations
2. Galbraith's Star Model
3. Jaques Stratification Systems Theory/Model.

### 1. *Mintzberg's Five Organisational Types/Configurations*

Lunenburg (2012) has identified Mintzberg's five organisational types or configurations including their application to various types of industries and organisations. Refer to Chapter 5.10 on creating separate organisational structures running parallel with the main organisation as an approach to going digital.

## Mintzberg's Five Organisational Types or Configurations

1. The Entrepreneurial Organisation: flat, relatively unstructured, flexible with a lack of standard systems, fast, lean but not appropriate when the organisation grows larger with the need to share power.

2. The Machine Organisation (bureaucracy): defined by standardisation with formalised work, routines and procedures, clearly defined jobs, centralised decision making and tasks grouped by functional departments with typically a tight vertical structure. However formalisation leads to specialisation with functional units having conflicting goals that may be inconsistent with overall corporate objectives (e.g., large manufacturers, government agencies and service firms that perform routine tasks).

3. The Professional Organisation: also bureaucratic but with a high degree of specialisation with decentralised decision making but nevertheless with lots of rules, typical of a large number of knowledge workers (e.g., universities, professional services firms).

4. The Divisional (Diversified) Organisation: many different product lines and business units with a central head office support, with each division having more control and accountability but on the flip side, there may be duplication of resources and activities, with divisions potentially in conflict competing with limited resources.

5. The Innovative Organisation (*Adhocracy*): suited to new industries where companies need to innovate and function on an *ad hoc* basis and where bureaucracy, complexity and centralisation are too limiting. Also suited to project based industries (e.g., film making, consulting). Whilst power is centralised, these organisations can be difficult to control. However these organisations help maintain a central pool of talent from which people can be drawn at any time to solve problems and work in a highly flexible way, with workers moving from team to team.

*2. Galbraith's Star Model*

Galbraith (2007) has developed a framework for organisational design based on a series of design policies incorporating five dimensions, all of which are inter-related.

> **Galbraith's Star Model**
>
> Galbraith's five dimensions include:
>
> 1. Strategy: which determines direction
> 2. Structure: which determines the location of decision-making power
> 3. Processes: which relate to the flow of information and the means of responding to information technologies
> 4. Rewards: which influence the motivation of people
> 5. People: which comprises HR policies and which influence and frequently define the employee's mindsets and skills.

These five dimensions are further discussed below.

## Strategy

Strategy specifies the goals and objectives to be achieved as well as the values and missions to be pursued. It sets out the basic direction of the organisation. It delineates the products and services to be provided, the markets to be served, the value to be offered to the customer, and the sources of competitive advantage of the organisation.

Strategy is critical in determining organisational form. Each organisational form enables some activities to be performed well, often at the expense of other activities.

Matrix organisations result when two or more activities must be accomplished without hindering the other. They require people who can manage conflict and influence without authority.

## Structure

The structure of an organisation determines the placement of power and authority in the organisation. Structural policies fall into four areas:

1. Specialisation: which refers to the type and numbers of job specialities
2. Shape: which refers to the number of people constituting the departments (span of control) at each level of the structure

    a. Distribution of power: which (in its vertical dimension) refers to the classic issues of centralisation versus decentralisation (see below)

    b. Departmentalisation: which is the basis of forming departments at each level of the structure (e.g., functions, products workflow processes, markets, customers, geography).

Structure affects status and power. However in a fast changing business world, and in matrix organisations, structure is becoming less important, while processes, rewards, and people are becoming more important.

## Processes

Information and decision processes cut across the organisation's structure. Management processes are both vertical and horizontal.

Vertical processes allocate resources of funds and talent and include business planning and budgeting processes, management approvals (where appropriate) and governance.

Horizontal (lateral) processes are designed around workflow (e.g. fulfilment of a customer order).

## Rewards

The purpose of rewards is to align goals of employees with the goals of the organisation and includes salaries, promotion, bonuses, profit sharing, share options, etc.

## People

People includes recruitment, training, rotation, development, etc., and produce the talent required by the strategy and structure of the organisation. HR policies build the organisational capabilities to execute the strategic direction.

For an organisation to be effective, all of the policies must be aligned and interact harmoniously with one another.

Culture and behaviour are influenced by management acting through the design policies.

*3. Jaques Stratification Systems Theory/Model*

Jaques developed a system and structural hierarchical framework of requisite organisation from his 'stratified systems theory', often referred to levels of work and running counter to many others in the field of organisational development. This model effectively limits the number of layers in an organisation but nevertheless it is a hierarchically based model.

> ### Jaques Stratification Systems Theory/Model
>
> Jaques is most widely known for his concept of the 'time-span of discretion'—a measure of how much responsibility an employee has. He argued that the higher a person was positioned in a hierarchy, assuming the individual possessed a corresponding level of cognitive complexity, acquired skills and knowledge (gained through experience), and presuming that individual valued the work he or she was tasked, the longer he could work to complete a task without supervision.
>
> The time span of a CEO of a major institution might be 15–20 years. This concept enabled him to describe a 'requisite organisation' as one in which each level in the hierarchy had its own distinctive time span. If an organisation had too many levels, then their time spans overlapped. If a manager at a higher level was ill equipped in respect of his or her inherent mental processing capability, or lacked the required skills and knowledge, the risk is that they would interfere in the work of managers at a lower level, generally propelled by their own anxiety and insecurity. The process of delegation would be undermined leading to organisational dysfunction.
>
> Effective hierarchy occurs when work at the next level is structured as focusing on the next level of complexity, and when leaders at the next level have one level higher capability (ability to deal with greater complexity) than their direct subordinates.

> With an understanding of mental processing capability and a hierarchy that supports the proficiency of work in the organisation, Jaques provided some insight into effective managerial practices that are aimed at freeing up the human potential in the organisation. For example, Jaques advocates the importance of effectively assigning tasks to individuals in the organisation delivered by contextualising the significance of the task(s) to the organisation's purpose in terms of output, including clear deliverables in respect of quantity, quality and the time for delivery. Moreover, a manager has an obligation to provide coaching to his or her subordinates, and the manager is in fact accountable for his or her subordinates' outputs.
>
> Jaques' work has often been met with criticism and the suggestion that a 'requisite organisation' provides a rigid and condescending structure that inhibits the performance of people within the organisation.

Whilst this model may be useful for the purposes of organisational design, including limiting hierarchy, it should not be used for workforce segmentation and HR reporting. Some 'Make' and 'Buy' roles will most probably be positioned on the same work level so lumping them together will result in jumbled reporting that will be difficult to interpret. For a further explanation, refer to Chapter 6, Step 5.

## Centralisation Versus Decentralisation

Most companies have centralised the activities surrounding the internet into a single unit to avoid fragmentation of activities and responses. In so doing, they have reduced duplication, achieved economies of scale, and presented one face to the customer. However on the down side, decision-making moves farther from the 'coal face' and work, with the central unit becoming an internal monopoly. Amongst other things, the result can be a lack of responsiveness to other departments that are using the internet.

## The Role of Product Manager

*The role of the Product Manager is expanding due to the growing importance of data in decision-making, an increased customer and design focus, and the evolution of software-development methodologies (Gnanasambandam, Harryson, Srivastava & Wu, 2017).*

Product Managers are central to the many functions that touch a product, from engineering, design, customer success, sales, marketing, operations, finance, legal and more. These Managers are responsible for what gets built and influence every aspect of how it gets built and launched. The Product Manager is in effect the mini-CEO of the product, wearing many hats, bringing together cross-functional teams, and ensuring alignment between diverse functions. It is important that organisations get the Product Manager role right in setting out to build software capabilities for success in the digital era.

**Note**. *The role of Product Manager is included in the Project Management Group in Chapter 6, Step 1.*

## Organisational Design Options in Digital Transformation

Organisational design options in digital transformation include:

- Running a separate yet parallel innovation team;
- Funding a separate company that becomes an innovation incubator; and
- The establishment of digital labs or pods that is separate to the main business, to digitise the new processes.

These options have been referred to earlier in Chapter 2 (on Innovation) and are further elaborated upon later in Chapter 5.12.

## 4.9 Leadership

Power (2017) has identified five essential characteristics that form the basis of successful leadership. These are outlined below.

---

**Power's Five Essential Leadership Characteristics**

1. Self-image
2. Self-control
3. Socialised power
4. Sustained dialogue
5. Strategic intent.

Through the leadership styles or leadership practices they demonstrate (or fail to demonstrate), leaders create the environment in which their staff will be motivated to provide discretionary effort. These five essential principles can be applied to leadership roles in any organisation, whether it be the largest of global corporations, a not-for-profit staffed entirely by volunteers.

*1. Self-image*

Effective leaders understand, believe and act upon a view of themselves that says, 'I am a leader'. Those in leadership positions who do not believe this of themselves tend to act more tentatively, indecisively, less confidently and with less impact than their more successful counterparts. This inability to assume the total persona of the role is reported to one of the greatest obstacles for people in leadership positions.

## 2. Self-control

Many leaders act on impulse, making decisions and taking action according to their habitual methods of dealing with situations, or reacting quickly in an attempt to solve a problem or to appear confident. The most effective leaders, however, tend to respond to situations rather than react to them. This degree of self-control, which is dependent on accurate self-awareness, allows leaders to be more effectively to manage their drives, values, personality traits, moods and preferences to meet the demands of different situations.

## 3. Socialised Power

Truly effective leaders create a vision to which others can commit, empower the members of the organisation to work responsibly toward attainment of that vision, hold them accountable for the outcome and acknowledge their efforts through considered recognition, praise and reward. This can be seen as the socialised or resourceful use of power, in contrast to a personalised or self-aggrandising abuse of power.

Leaders who exercise power in this way help others improve, bring conflict out into the open in a constructive way and help to resolve it for the benefit of all. They find common ground with others, have a network in place when it is time for action and collaborate willingly across boundaries. Their approach to leadership is authoritative, not authoritarian, and they involve people in the work by engagement rather than coercion.

## 4. Sustained Dialogue

It is easy for a leader, especially someone new to the role, to bunker down and focus on understanding and managing the things they need to achieve, just as they did in the roles that brought them to this level in the first place. The best leaders, however, make a point of getting out and about to meet their team and the rest of the staff of the organisation.

They create every possible opportunity to speak with their people, not as a friend, but as a senior colleague who is there to encourage, mentor and support them, and to provide the resources and the environment in which they can do their best work. This helps the leader to develop a level of true empathy with those who work for the organisation, so that they are regarded as people rather than cogs in the organisational machine. It also improves the quality of performance management, and builds better cooperation and collaboration. People who are skilled in using their 'social radar' are better able to observe and listen to others, and seek to understand why they act as they do.

Barriers that operate for many leaders include ignorance of differences, stereotyping of others according to race, ethnicity, socioeconomic status, religion, colour, gender or other such characteristics, expectations of others, either positive or negative, that can help shape their behaviour, narcissism, self-centredness and unconscious biases.

**5. *Strategic Intent***

Leaders typically find themselves in a senior role because they have been high-achievers in their current organisations, or in other organisations. It is reasonable for them to assume, therefore, that they will achieve success in their new role by doing more of the same. This unfortunately generates an attitude of being hands-on, keeping a close eye on others, focusing on the minutiae, to the extent of micro-managing and even taking credit for the team's successes. Proper leadership involvement is not a bad thing, as it lends itself to the parts of the role that require planning, goal-setting, prioritising and strategising. Having developed the strategy, unfortunately some leaders do not step back to maintain perspective. Rather, they tend to lose perspective in the pursuit of short-term, tactical goals. Effective leaders recognise that they need to keep watch on the big picture, and take a broader and long-term view as they continue to create and articulate a compelling vision.

> They keep others and themselves focused on it to the extent that everything that happens in the organisation can be tied to its overall mission. People understand clearly how what they do on a day-to-day basis contributes to that wider, long-term plan. These leaders derive an unwavering sense of purpose and bring a real passion to it, which in turn, inspires commitment and engagement from others.
>
> Good leaders make the complex simple through strategic intent. People are free to do their best when the strategic choices have been made clear, and this results in a clear connection between chosen activities and outcomes. When colleagues participate in strategy creation, and when strategic intent is made clear, they have less reason to check with the leader and more reason to do their best to reach the goals. Delegation becomes easier and more effective.

## Leadership Models and Innovative Companies

*Leaders matter but leadership matters more with building collective leadership depth throughout the organisation (Ulrich, 2017).*

There are many different leadership models, including:

- Situational;
- Transformative;
- Participative;
- Visionary;
- Affiliative;
- Blue Ocean, etc.

A detailed analysis of these various leadership styles is beyond the scope of this book. That said, according to Gregersen (2017) from the MIT Leadership Centre, the most effective innovative companies show the following five leadership characteristics.

> ### MIT Leadership Centre: Five Characteristics of Innovative Companies
>
> 1. Questioning: provoking the *status quo* unrelentingly, challenging existing thinking and operational paradigms
> 2. Observing: immersing in people and processes in the business including external stakeholders to gain a first had experience of products and services
> 3. Networking: establishing extensive and broad relationships and networks to promote divergent thinking and radical ideas from outside their existing realm of expertise and experience
> 4. Experimenting: to testing and trialing ideas and concepts
> 5. Associating: making connections between people, ideas, across industries, drawing new insights from these associations.
>
> This combination of character and skills ensures that leaders are working in the business, on the business, and for the future business, sharpening insights and challenging colleagues

## Leadership and Achieving Digital Sustainability

*Leaders must demonstrate to the organisation that the (digital transformation) journey is directional and the journey itself will provide the opportunities to define the future (Reimer, Feuerstein, Meighan & Kelly, 2017).*

> **Korn Ferry Five Leadership Characteristics to Achieve Digital Sustainability**
>
> According to Korn Ferry (2017), to achieve digital sustainability, the following five leadership and organisational capabilities are essential:
>
> 1. Discipline and focus
> 2. Agility
> 3. Connectivity
> 4. Openness and transparency
> 5. Empowerment and alignment.

As referred to earlier, leadership should support and drive the entire organisation to adopt a dynamic, data-driven culture. Digital sustainability requires new skills, competencies and ways of working and significant investment in effective change management to embed the 'new normal' into the organisation's culture, ethics, values, beliefs, processes and practices. 'Fit for purpose' is no longer good enough – organisations and leaders need to become fit-for-future!

# 4.10 Culture

**Characteristics of Organisational Culture**

> *BusinessDictionary.com defines culture as: The pattern of responses discovered, developed, or invented during the group's history of handling problems which arise from interactions amongst its members, and between them and their environment. These*

*responses are considered the correct way to perceive, think, and act, and are passed on to the new members through immersion and teaching. Culture determines what is acceptable or unacceptable, important or unimportant, right or wrong, workable or unworkable. It encompasses all learned and shared, explicit or tacit, assumptions, beliefs, knowledge, norms, and values, as well as attitudes, behaviour, dress, and language.*

Culture is a multi-faceted and somewhat elusive concept with the characteristics of culture including the following:

- Powerful and mysterious, hard to define, hard to change;
- The emotional centre, the heartbeat of the enterprise and unique to that enterprise;
- An outcome of what the entire organisation (i.e., its people) focuses its minds and energies on;
- Organic, that blossoms, changes or fades over time;
- An undeniable force that defines how employees and customers are treated, and how goals are achieved;
- It exists, whether it is known or recognised as such, and can be diagnosed;
- It can be changed by choosing to amplify those elements that are aligned to the strategy and delivering business results, or changing processes or systems to define and reinforce desired behaviours;
- Includes norms and behaviours that are rewarded and discouraged by the people and processes within the organisation.

Culture is a team sport, not a HR responsibility, but HR has a role to play in shaping culture.

## Culture and Leadership

Culture is the one constant in a volatile and unpredictable future. Trust in leaders is a vital element of culture. Developing a common mission and sense of belonging in an increasingly dispersed workforce is also crucially important in developing a favourable culture.

Leaders must be developed so that they can ultimately influence culture, including creating a culture where innovation thrives. You can't overhaul your platforms and solutions without changing your culture and thinking. Organisations must therefore embed the ability to change into their DNA: into their practices and processes, culture, values, beliefs and into mindset of their entire workforce.

## Building a Digital Culture

Organisations today need to develop a self-sustaining culture and infrastructure to continually adapt and thrive in the digital economy. They must develop a clear digital strategy, and a cultural mindset of risk, openness, experimentation, and digital skills. Collaboration, agility, and digital innovation are characteristics of a digital-first culture.

Furthermore, the characteristics that define a digital intelligence culture start with being inquisitive and seeking out data that will provide new insight. They include basing decisions on evidence over leaders' experience-based wisdom or 'gut feel.' A digital intelligence culture has a bias for action, favouring experimentation that itself is tracked, analysed, and then iterated upon.

Such a culture and mindset can be fostered by a variety of initiatives including: educating, training, and stimulating employees with digital seminars, road shows, education programs, and partner days. It must also be supported by the right policies, infrastructure and tools. Instruction and training with the new technology and processes should also be provided.

Successful digital transformation depends on getting people on board. One of the biggest risks is that employees fail to adapt to the new technology and digital processes. Crucial at any stage of digital transformation is the need for an emphasis on change management (refer later to Chapter 6, Step 8).

For HR, developing a digital culture and digital intelligence means rethinking processes and measures of the organisation's human resources to optimise the digital strategy including:

- Organisational design and structures that accelerate information flows, collaboration and innovation;
- Talent acquisition and development initiatives that actively source and build the digital skills needed by the organisation's workforce;
- Key performance indicators that align individual contributions with business outcomes; and
- Embracing HR technologies and analytics to underpin human capital strategies.

Refer to Chapter 7 on the extended role of the HR Director/Manager and to Chapter 8 on Developing a Digital Workplace Strategy.

## 4.11 People Management Practices in Digital Organisations

### The Importance of the People Factor

Competitive advantage in the digital age not only lies with the best technology, but in using and mastering talent well. People are at the heart of the digital economy—their primacy remains. They will still be the driving force and arguably the most important element in making a digital transformation useful, successful, and valuable. The digital culture shock and deep disruption is a permanent feature of the competitive landscape. While digital disruption is a threat to established industries and market leaders, it is also an opportunity to re-engage the workforce, drive innovation, reduce costs, attract talent, boost efficiency and thrive in an increasingly global and disruptive competitive landscape.

However many companies focus their transformation efforts on IT and business processes, too often neglecting people. Changing customer expectations and accelerating disruption demand digital business agility—the capacity of an organisation to understand and react to digital threats and opportunities. The workforce is a critical component of digital business agility.

### Management Practices of Digital Organisations

There is a shift in emphasis of the management practices of 'digital organisations' compared to more traditional businesses. Whilst integrated talent management is still important, employee engagement, teamwork, innovation, and collaboration have emerged as key people management issues. There is a focus on:

- Reinventing how people work;
- Creating team-based tools for goal alignment and coaching;
- Putting in place systems to provide feedback and measure engagement;

- Rethinking the way performance is measured, careers are managed, and individual learning enabled; and
- Enhancing the employee experience over the employment life cycle.

Employers will become more employee-centric. People management practices relating to the above are elaborated upon below.

Notwithstanding these shifts in people management practices, in the workplace of the future there are issues about surveillance, monitoring, and privacy, with a network of cameras and sensors. In other words, how much information about individuals and their digital trail should be available, to whom, and for what purpose?

## Performance Management

Performance and engagement management is shifting from a centralized model facilitated by HR to a decentralized model conducted by managers, that has increased management accountability. Leading companies are now reinventing the way they manage and measure performance, creating a more agile approach built around:

- Periodic check-ins;
- Shared goals that are developed from the bottom up and transparent to the entire team;
- Regular developmental conversations; and
- Multi-directional feedback that goes from employee to employee, employee to manager, and manager to employee.

The issue of ratings in performance management has been a controversial one in recent times. Dissatisfaction has been expressed by both managers and employees, including the difficulties of judging people, having honest two way conversations, consistency of measurement, etc. Most companies have dispensed with an employee relativity or comparison rating system. Others have experimented with the abandonment of a rating system altogether, whilst some have sought to replace one rating system with an alternative *de facto* one. Some have shifted their focus from an annual conversation to improving the frequency and quality of their coaching, while others have sought to de-emphasise the link between pay and performance.

According to recent research by CEB (2016), the business case for removing performance ratings does not hold. Their study of 10,000 employees from 18 countries confirmed that there was no increase in employee engagement with the removal of ratings. Expectations of more informal coaching failed to materialise, the quality of feedback from managers was worse, expectations of fairer pay were worse, and high performers were more disengaged when ratings were abolished. These findings are a salutary reminder of HR adopting the latest fad or whim, without an evidenced based approach.

*You can't manage what you don't measure!*

Performance management may be changing as part of an ongoing feedback mechanism rather than a once a year event. Care should be exercised to ensure that technology isn't regarded as a 'panacea', introduced to support more frequent and real-time feedback, but ending up replacing face-to-face conversations.

Ultimately people performance needs to be measured, like any other output that impacts on the bottom line. Like it or not, people are continually being judged on their performance, whether it's in the sporting field, or in the workplace. In a matrix organisation, there may be more than one person involved in assessing performance. Performance management is actually much more about execution and much less about system design. It is here to stay, although its application and frequency of use may be subject to a different emphasis.

## Engagement

Organisations are adapting to new ways of attracting, engaging and managing talent. Engagement includes, amongst other things, the following elements:

- To the organisation: its purpose, vision, mission, and goals;
- To the job: its functions, challenges, autonomy, resources (including technology), training, development opportunities and rewards and benefits;
- To the people (social): to the personal and professional relationships, collaboration, support and teamwork;
- To the structure: the policies, practices (including flexibility) and environment.

Another major shift in people management is a new understanding that feedback and 'always-on' engagement measurement are important to business success. Today tools are available that allow companies to:

- Deploy pulse surveys;
- Provide feedback to teams and managers;
- Create open, anonymous networks; and
- Analyse employees' comments and free form text.

These tools are identifying management problems, leadership gaps, safety and compliance issues, and fraud and theft problems never before made visible. Furthermore there are difficulties in tracking and responding to quarterly and monthly changes in perceptions with the typical annual employee survey. Just as it would be unthinkable to measure an organisation's financial and customer performance only once a year, so is the case with a sole reliance on an annual employee survey to measure engagement.

That said, there is still a place for the more comprehensive employee survey across the whole workforce (or a significant sample of the workforce) in order to identify and differentiate:

- Wider organisational issues;
- Business Unit issues;
- Local workplace issues.

Targeted interventions are then able to be directed to address 'hot spots' starting with a top down approach for maximum impact.

Thus the traditional annual engagement survey can be augmented with other forms of feedback collection to capture and measure employees' perceptions, feelings, opinions and ideas in an environment of rapid pace of change. The combination of quantitative and qualitative metrics, organisations are able to build a more complete view of the employee experience.

## A New Focus on the Employee Experience

*As Susan Peters (as in Meister2017), Senior Vice President, Human Resources at General Electric says, 'We define employee experience simply as seeing the world through the eyes of our employees, staying connected, and being aware of their major milestones'.*

Employee experience has taken off recently as a hot topic which is not only about attracting talent, but aimed at keeping talent engaged and productive for longer. Some may contend this new emphasis constitutes 'old wine in new bottles'. As in the case of the new emphasis on customer experience, these experiences and relationships that follow, constitute levers of competitive advantage for organisations. Employees are increasingly expecting a similar experience at work to that which they receive as a customer. One way of capturing this experience is through employee journey mapping over the employment life cycle, applying a consumer and a digital lens to gain a better understanding of their motivations and expectations. Employee want an experience and not just a job!

*Note. Refer earlier to Chapter 1.4 regarding reference to customer journeys that is essentially the same concept as applied to employee journeys.*

The employee experience includes a holistic focus that considers all the contributors to worker satisfaction, engagement, wellness, and alignment. A new marketplace of pulse feedback tools, wellness and fitness apps, and integrated, employee self-service tools is helping HR departments understand and improve this experience. Developing an integrated employee experience across the above multiple dimensions requires HR and business leaders to combine insights in all of these areas. This also involves targeting to the various needs of different employees, which raises complexity and equity challenges.

*Bersin by Deloitte (2017) defines the talent relationship thus: The systematic relationship with talent is defined as the systems and processes that enable multi-directional interactions and exchanges of information, ideas, resources and needs between employees and the organisation, as well as approaches for the organisation to analyse that information and respond appropriately at scale.*

The fostering of this talent relationship requires an increased engagement with employees. The end goal is to create a talent experience that results in employees feeling heard, valued, and supported throughout their entire time with an organisation (i.e., throughout the employment life cycle). Employees' expectations revolve around the concepts of ease and flexibility. They want easy to use modern technology (including its mobile adoption), and access work related documents and information at any time from any place. These themes are elaborated upon later in Chapter 8.

## 4.12 The Agile Organisation

### An Introduction to Agile

*Note.* A brief overview of Agile is provided below. The various practices and frameworks incorporated in Agile when applied to software development is a specialized area beyond the scope of this book.

Agile is the topic *du jour!* It is most commonly referenced in relation to project management, especially within software development. The shift to Agile is driven by proof that small, multidisciplinary teams of agile organisations can respond swiftly and promptly to rapidly changing market opportunities and customer demands. Agile efforts are focused on creating working software – incremental software product versions that can be tested at the system level and demonstrated to the customer. It is characterized by the division of tasks into short sprints of work with regular assessment and adaptation, and incremental releases of work.

Unlike the traditional waterfall method, which stipulates lengthy requirements-gathering processes and long development cycles, Agile encourages short development cycles using cross functional teams. Progress is mapped visually and reported on regularly, often through stand up meetings.

Agile follows the empirical process control model for delivering high quality products well within the timelines – by frequent inspection, reflection and adaptation of its processes. By doing so, Agile teams become better at their internal processes – communication, decision making, problem solving, etc.

Agile needs close collaboration with the customer throughout the project tenure, making sure that the customer gets what he/she wants. Agile methods have built-in processes to change their plans at regular intervals based on feedback from customers. Agile methodologies are based on the knowledge that, in order to succeed, Agile teams must plan to change and adapt. These teams are built around end-to-end accountability with hierarchy stripped down. Leadership shows direction and enables action.

## The Heart of Agile

At the heart of Agile, lies its manifesto and principles. The mindset of Agile includes the switch from:

- Profits to Purpose;
- Hierarchies to Networks;
- Controlling to Empowering;
- Planning to Experimentation;
- Privacy to Transparency.

The foundational practices of Agile are:

- Set a direction and purpose;
- Create information transparency;
- Accelerate decision making;
- Empower teams.

The core values of Agile are:

- Trust;
- Respect;
- Transparency;
- Truth;
- Commitment.

Of the above core values, trust is arguably the most significant. One can replace structure with 'squads', 'tribes' and 'chapters', and one can introduce daily stand up meetings and scrum like habits and introduce agile coaches to support the ways of working. But ultimately its about behavior and intentions.

The Agile way of working assumes autonomy. Autonomy can only work if there is trust which involves, amongst other things:

- Integrity, honesty and truthfulness;
- Competence;
- Consistency, reliability, predictability and good judgement;
- Loyalty; and
- Openness, willingness to share information.

So it is important to have all of these elements or aspects of trust partly in place before embarking on an Agile approach.

Furthermore, traditional organisations are designed as siloed hierarchies based on a mindset of authority. The relationship between leaders and teams is one of superior to subordinate. People lower down the ladder defer to and comply with the wishes of people at more senior levels. In return leaders protects and reward their people.

However Agile is the anthesis of hierarchy. Designed for collaboration, Agile organisations employee networks of autonomous teams. This requires an underlying mindset of partnership – managing by agreement. Agile leaders need to find ways of balancing steering and supporting. Agile teams are largely self-governing with senior leaders telling members where to innovate but not how.

In summary, Agile is a leadership distribution model, connecting autonomous teams with a high degree of flexibility.

## Where Agile Best Fits in an Organisation

As referred to earlier, it is more important than ever for organisations to respond quickly to changing customer needs and requirements – to reconfigure strategy, structure, processes, people and technology toward value-creating and value-protecting opportunities.

However some companies struggle to know which functions should be reorganised into Agile teams and which functions should not. Not every function needs to be organised into Agile teams - even the most Agile teams operate with a mix of Agile teams and traditional organisational structures.

The Agile organisation can be conceived in terms of the different types of building blocks of work.

| Agile Building Block | Description | Application |
| --- | --- | --- |
| 1. Cross functional teams | Teams composed of different functional expertise from different levels, typically including a product or project owner | Product development |
| 2. Self-managing teams | Stable teams – typically repetitive work delivering base load activity | Customer services, sales, manufacturing |
| 3. 'Flow to work' pools | Pool of individuals (SMEs) staffed to different tasks, based on priority needs | Corporate services (HR, legal, IT) |

It is in 1. Cross Functional Teams, where Agile modular approaches are best applied. These typically include three components:

1. Customer experience teams – that identifies all the experience that could significantly affect internal and external and internal customer decisions, behaviours and satisfaction.
2. Business process teams - examines the relationship between these experiences and key business processes, aiming to reduce overlapping responsibilities and increase collaboration between process and customer experience teams.
3. Technology teams - focuses on developing technology systems to improve the processes that will support customer experience teams.

Initially these components operate as discrete sets of teams, but then there is a need to integrate them. The leadership team sets priorities and sequences decisions. Leaders must consider multiple criteria including:

- Strategies importance;
- Budget limitations;
- Availability of people;
- Return on investment;
- Interdependencies amongst teams.

The most importance are the pain points felts by customers and employees felt on the one hand, and the organisations capabilities and constraints on the other.

## Agile Applied to the Wider Organisation

There is a growing number of public sector leaders who see the need to deliver faster and perform in a way that is more relevant to user demand. Top down models have given way to user driven models. The community is expecting more and more as traditional institutions struggle to deliver. These expectations of citizens/community/members will be difficult to meet without the adoption of new methods of delivery.

*Speed is the new business currency with rapid innovation having become a strategic imperative for many companies.*

Though Agile is largely practised as a software development approach, today many practitioners believe that Agile is meant for and can evolve into a powerful cultural and business paradigm. Thus Agile approaches have given rise to broader applications yielding transformation and impact across an entire enterprise. It is being hailed as the new order for organisations to unlock value in an uncertain and rapidly changing environment. The advantage of Agile are clear – faster processes, a more rewarding work culture, and enhanced flexibility.

The term Agile has now expanded into many facets of solution development with the same underlying principles:

- Develop iteratively;
- Release frequently;

- Customer focus;
- Collaborate through cross functional teams.

Test and learn methods take priority over detailed planning, with the ability to work well in parallel and to minimize the number of decision or alignment choke points. However changes are necessary to ensure that functions that don't operated as agile teams support the ones that do. There is a change process that organisations must go through.

The Agile organisation is dawning as the new organisational paradigm - being understood as a living organism. Whilst transforming organisations to achieve organisational agility is on the rise, it's still in its early days.

*Note. AWS has developed a Program entitled 'Enhancing Organisational Agility and Customer Centricity'. This Program includes a workshop entitled 'Embracing the Future' for managers and staff that addresses themes such as: Digital Transformation, Agility, Customer Centricity, Workplace Trends, Skills Required for the Future. There are a series of practical activities that participants work through applying these themes to themselves and their own work places.*

## Agile Structures

The typical agile company employs a dynamic matrix structure with two types of reporting lines:

1. A capability line (chapters)
2. A value-creation line (squads and tribes).

Nearly all employees have both a functional reporting line, which is their long-term home in the company, and a value-creation reporting line, which sets the objectives and business needs they take on in squads.

### *Squads (Scrum Teams)*

Squads are small teams, that have a great deal of autonomy. Typically composed of eight to ten developers of different skills sets or capabilities, they have end-to-end accountability for specific outcomes and make their own decisions about how to achieve their goals.

*Chapters*

The capability reporting lines are often called 'chapters' and are similar in some ways to functions in traditional organisations. Each chapter is responsible for building a particular capability (e.g., user experience, ERP) including: hiring, firing, developing talent, shepherding people along their career paths, evaluating and promoting people, and building standard tools, methods, and ways of working.

The chapters also must deploy their talented people to the appropriate squads, based on their expertise and demonstrated competence. In essence, chapters are responsible for the 'how' of a company's work. However, once talent is deployed to an agile team (i.e., squad), the chapters do not tell people what to work on, nor do they set priorities, assign work or tasks, or supervise the day-to-day activities.

*Tribes (comprising groups of Squads)*

The value-creation reporting lines are often called 'tribes.' They focus on making money and delivering value to customers (e.g., a 'mortgage services' tribe or a 'mobile products' tribe). Tribes are similar to business units or product lines in traditional organisations. Tribes essentially 'rent' most of their resources from the chapters. If chapters are responsible for the 'how,' tribes are responsible for the 'what.' They set priorities and objectives and provide marching orders to the functional resources deployed to them.

*Guilds*

A guild is a community of members with shared interests. They are comprised of a group of people from across the organisation who want to share knowledge, tools code and practices. Each guild has a co-coordinator, and such guilds include: web technology guild, test automation guild or even an agile coaching guild.

## Agile Roles

*The Chapter Leader*

This chapter leader must build up the right capabilities and people, equip them with the skills, tools, and standard approaches to deliver functional excellence, and ensure that they are deployed to value-creation opportunities—sometimes in long-term roles supporting the business, but more often to the small, independent squads. The chapter leader must evaluate, promote, coach, and develop his or her people, but without traditional direct oversight. Chapter leaders are not involved in the day-to-day work of squads; they don't check on or approve the work of their chapter members, and they certainly don't micromanage or provide daily oversight. Instead, regular feedback from tribe leaders, team members, and other colleagues inform their evaluations and the kind of coaching they provide. Since they're not providing direct oversight, their span of control can expand greatly, a fact that can eliminate several layers of management. In fact, chapter leaders often free up enough time to tackle 'real work' on business opportunities as well.

*The Tribe Leader*

Since these value-creation leaders borrow or rent most of their resources from the chapters, they no longer bear the burden of building up their own functional capabilities. Instead, tribe leaders act as true general managers, mini-CEOs focused on value creation, growth, and serving customers. They must develop the right strategies and tactics to deliver desired business outcomes and to determine what work needs to get done, how much to invest in which efforts, and how to prioritize opportunities. They work with chapter leaders to match the right people to the right squads.

*The Squad Leader/Scrum Master*

Team leaders, or 'squad' leaders, serve a crucial purpose in the agile matrix. They aren't the 'boss' of the people on their team – rather they are servant leaders. They support the development team, clearing organisational roadblocks, and keeping the agile process consistent. They help plan and orchestrate execution of the work, scheduling and leading sprint meetings, keeping the team productive, and they strive to build a cohesive team. They also provide inspiration, coaching, and feedback to team members, report back on progress to tribe leaders, and give input on people development and performance to relevant chapter leaders. They are most effective when they have organisational clout, which is the ability to influence change in the organisation without formal authority.

*Product Owner*

The product owner, who is part of the squad, represents the voice of the customer and is in charge of the story prioritisation. This person is responsible for bridging the gap between the customer, business stakeholders, and the development team. The product owner is an expert on the product and the customer's needs and priorities. This person works with the development team daily to help clarify requirements and shields them from organisational noise. The product owner is sometimes called a customer representative. The product owner, above all, should be empowered to be decisive, making tough business decisions every day.

*Development Team Members (Squad Team or Scrum Team Members)*

These are the people who create the product. In software development, programmers, testers, designers, writers, data engineers, and anyone else with a hands-on role in product development are development team members. Most importantly, development team members should be versatile, able to contribute in multiple ways to the project's goals.

*Agile Mentor/Coach*

An Agile mentor or coach is someone who has experience implementing agile projects and can share that experience with a squad. The Agile mentor can provide valuable feedback and advice to new squads and to squads that want to perform at a higher level. Although Agile mentors are not responsible for executing product development, they should be experienced in applying Agile principles in reality and be knowledgeable about many Agile approaches and techniques.

Chapter 5

# Digital Transformation

## 5.1 Digital: The New Way of Doing Things

As highlighted in Chapter 1, *Digital is the New Universe*, it is the new way of doing things. Digitisation impacts all business models, sooner or later and should be integrated into all aspects of the business, including the strategic planning process. It requires a broader view about the business envisioning new value for clients. There is a need to deeply understand how customers derive value from the provision of products and services.

Many people think having a few digital initiatives in the air constitutes a digital strategy – it does not! Some view digital as an upgraded term for what their IT function does. Others focus on digital marketing or sales. Very few have a comprehensive or holistic view of what digital means.

The process of becoming a truly digital enterprise extends operationally, strategically and culturally across every facet of the organisation. It demands the complete transformation of operating models, workflows, supply chains and service delivery. Organisations must disrupt legacy systems and hierarchies to become digitally sustainable, transforming into open, interconnected networks populated by a fluid workforce and led by a new profile leader. It requires the strategic alignment of capabilities across the entire organisation. Investment in technology and the development and/or acquisition of digital skills is just the beginning of an organisation's transformation journey.

There are four key dimensions of digital transformation involving:

1. People, culture and structure
2. Business and digital strategies and associated processes
3. Technology platforms and systems
4. Measurement and management information systems.

This Book is more focused on (1) people, culture and structure, with the other three dimensions given somewhat cursory attention.

Preparing any large organisation to capitalise on digital opportunities is no small feat. Changes to the business model means changes to the shape of the workforce. It is mission-critical to anticipate how changing strategies and business models will alter an organisation's workforce requirements. Now more than ever before, the corporate strategy for large companies hinges on their people strategies. Whatever technological innovations are ahead, it's people that will make the difference, which is why organisations need a people or workforce strategy.

## 5.2 What is Digital Transformation?

*CIO (2017) defines digital transformation as: The acceleration of business activities, processes, competencies, and models to fully leverage the changes and opportunities of digital technologies and their impact in a strategic and prioritised way.*

Digital transformation is about the fusion of these two disparate domains to improve performance and services that an organisation provides:

1. Information Technology (IT)
2. The business.

Digital transformation is the realignment of or new investment in technology, business models and processes to drive new value and improve the experience of customers, employees, partners, and stakeholders to compete more efficiently in an ever-changing digital economy.

That said, digital transformation is still in its infancy and it carries different connotations depending on the nature of the business. There is no one model of digital transformation, nor is there any one technology that must be used to achieve it. But more than just acceleration, digital transformation is about the need for businesses to outpace digital disruption and stay competitive in a rapidly evolving business environment. As referred to earlier, essential to digital transformation is the development of new competencies that revolve around the capacities to be more agile, people-oriented, innovative, customer-centric, aligned and efficient, with present and future shifts in mind.

The end goals of the business, customers and stakeholders drive the agenda. The central role of the organisation is to connect the dots and overcome internal silos in all areas in order to reach these different goals with interconnectedness being the norm.

A key digital transformation question for business is: *How can digital services best be wrapped around existing products and services, including launching new ones that capture customers, and find innovative ways to act, both externally and internally?*

## 5.3 The Goals of Digital Transformation

According to TRA (2016), the top five goals of digital transformation strategies are:

1. Accelerating time to market
2. Streamlining and optimising operations
3. Creating more innovative IT platforms (including a lack of flexibility in technology environments)
4. Reducing and optimising costs
5. Improving customer experience and engagement.

These top five competitive pressures are a mix of both external market and internal technology factors. The technology factors organisations identified by TRA as being integral to their business transformation programme, in order of importance were:

- Migration to the cloud;
- Data management; and
- Enterprise mobility.

## 5.4 Impacts of Digital Transformation

Digital transformation in the integrated and connected sense that it requires, can impact upon the transformation of:

- Business activities/functions: Marketing, operations, human resources, administration, customer service, etc.
- Business processes: One or more connected operations, activities and sets to achieve a specific business goal that may include business process management, business process optimisation and business process automation.
- Business models: How businesses function, from the go-to-market approach and

value proposition to the ways they seek to make money and effectively transform their core business, tapping into novel revenue sources and approaches, sometimes even dropping the traditional core business after a while.

- Business ecosystems: The networks of partners and stakeholders, as well as contextual factors affecting the business such as regulatory or economic priorities and evolutions.
- Business asset management: Whereby the focus lies on traditional assets but, increasingly, on less tangible assets such as information and customers (enhancing customer experience is a leading goal of many digital transformation projects and information is the lifeblood of business, technological evolutions and of any human relationship).
- Organisational culture: Whereby there is a clear customer-centric, agile and hyper-aware goal that is achieved by acquiring core competencies across the board in areas such as digital maturity, leadership, knowledge, worker silos and so forth.
- Ecosystem and partnership models: With amongst others, a rise of co-operative, collaborative, co-creating and, last but not least, entirely new business ecosystem approaches, leading to new business models and revenue sources.
- Customer, worker and partner approaches: Whereby digital transformation puts people and strategy before technology. The changing behaviour, expectations and needs of any stakeholder are crucial. This is expressed in many change subprojects that can include considerations of customer-centricity, user experience, worker empowerment, new workplace models, changing channel partner dynamics etc.

*Note.* *It's important to note that digital technologies are never the sole answer to tackle any of these human aspects, from worker satisfaction to customer experience enhancement. People involve, respect and empower other people in the first place. Technology is an additional enabler.*

Just as social business, digital business and any form of customer-centric marketing and business processes require the ability to work across silos. In many cases, digital transformation, apart from totally reworking organisational structures and removing silos, can be as much about collaborative methods.

## 5.5 Digital Transformation Isn't Cheap

Digital business transformation isn't cheap! It is a major investment. Leading firms are spending hundreds of millions of dollars to overhaul all aspects of their businesses to become customer-centric and digital to the core. There are no shortcuts!

Large scale transformation is a multiyear proposition demanding approval at the highest level. Front end initiatives require improvements to the core systems that underpin them including streamlining processes and removing redundancy across the organisation. According to Beeson (2017), organisations may need to spend $4 on digital operational excellence for every $1 spent on digital customer experiences.

Adopting a test-and-learn approach to rolling out digital initiatives is a proven way of identifying the key cross-touch point experiences that make the most difference to a firm's bottom line. Proof of concepts should be adopted wherever possible. Speed to market and experimentation are the cornerstones of digital business transformation.

## 5.6 Phases of Digitisation

Digital changes can be categorised according to: (1) product, (2) channel, and/or (3) operations, ranging from enhancement to transformational. The earlier phases of digitisation focused more heavily on operations than on products and channels, with the latter becoming a prime focus in more recent times. Customer facing digital channels include mobile applications and web portals.

| Phases of Digitisation | Enhancement | Transformation |
| --- | --- | --- |
| Products: Changes to products or services port folio | Using data and technology to enhance existing products and services | Launching new products or services beyond the core business portfolio |
| Channels: Changes to sales, marketing, and customer service capabilities | Improving channel coordination and performance | Transforming channels to match customer behaviours and preferences |
| Operations: Changes to other business capabilities | Improving productivity or optimising enterprise activities and processes | Making broad improvements in one or more corporate functions |

Within the above phases, the progress or stage of digital transformation can be classified as either:

- Not developed;
- In development;
- Deployed in part;
- Deployed in full;
- Undergoing evaluation;
- Undergoing continual improvement.

## 5.7 Five Levels of Digital Transformation

Holliday (2017) contends that there are five very distinct levels of innovation relating to digital transformation that occur within organisations. These levels and their characteristics are described below.

## Holiday's Five Levels of Innovation in Digital Transformation

*Level 1: Stagnating*

- Characterised by an analogue operating system, legacy products and services;
- A key focus is on maintaining the *status quo*;
- Internal effort is focused on reinforcing the past to guarantee the future;
- Likely to have low digital literacy at an executive level.

*Level 2: Reformatting*

- Characterised by transferring existing ideas and products to a digital medium;
- A key focus is on rebranding and repackaging legacy products and services;
- Internal efforts are focused on process improvement;
- Moving assets and processes across to a digital medium, focusing on digital to do existing things faster and cheaper.

**Note.** *Most digital transformations are at this level.*

*Level 3: Inquiry*

- Characterised by new ideas and technology (platforms);
- Recognise that the standard approach is no longer working and that the climate is fundamentally different;
- Need to stop and reassess long held beliefs;
- Connect to a deep sense of purpose;
- Likely to have higher digital literacy.

*Note. Connecting to a deeper sense of purpose is more than a profit only focus. It's about defining the 'superordinate why' that the organisation offers, linking its products and services to a broader perspective.*

*Level 4: Transforming*

- Characterised by some real action;
- Businesses start to reconstitute their assets in new and creative ways, combining and repositioning them to create new products, services, partnerships;
- This level activates a resetting of the business life cycle;
- New organisational forms emerge, new ways of working, silos are replaced by networks/teams that work cross functionally and collaboratively.

> *Level 5: Redefining*
>
> - Characterised by whole system, DNA innovation (purpose, people, product, platform, process);
> - Home of the emergent organisation;
> - Self-organisation and innovation takes place;
> - Organisations are ecosystems, constantly rearranging themselves around the customer.
>
> **Note.** *Very few organisations attain this level.*

## 5.8 Platform Ecosystems, the Cloud & Digital Transformation

*A platform is a system that creates value by facilitating relationships between consumers and producers.*

Until recently, a 'platform' was something people stood on. On a more serious note, digital platforms are software layers that gather and synthesis large volumes of data to make digital services accessible and available on various devices. They help define rules, better coordinate activities and lower costs. In practice, platforms typically take the form of a website, app or other digital tool that connects different types of users.

Now every tech start-up under the sun claims to offer a 'platform' so the term has become muddled. Unlike a market place that allows anyone to sell anything, a platform essentially takes responsibility for the quality and type of products or services exchanged. Platforms are the new ways of connecting people and products/services.

The holy grail of an online business is to make an organisation a platform for wider value creation within the digital ecosystems that extends well beyond traditional geographies, and in ways that enable it to collect revenue.

Cloud-based platforms remove the need to maintain servers, patch and update systems. The benefits of cloud access outweigh the benefits of ownership. The cloud ecosystem is foundational with future technology innovations increasingly being delivered by the cloud. Refer later to Chapter 8 and 9 for further discussion on the cloud.

## 5.9 Mastering Digital Customer Experience & Operational Excellence

> *Digital businesses win, serve, and retain customers by continuously creating and exploiting digital assets to simultaneously deliver new sources of customer value and increase their operational agility.*

Organisations must begin to look at digital holistically and transform by applying digital thinking across everything they do including:

- How they win, serve, and retain customers;
- How they operate internal processes; and
- How they source business services.

There are two dimensions of digital that should be pursued in parallel:

1. Digital customer experience
2. Digital operational excellence.

Organisations are able to use technologies to improve processes and create new products, services and channels to market. Digital transformation efforts can lead to costs savings and greater innovation. E-commerce and digital processes are progressively becoming more important to business, with more companies going digital. As referred to previously, the revolution of digitisation is fundamentally changing the way many companies make and sell products, as well as reaching customers/consumers.

## 5.10 Going Digital Is a 'Mixed Bag'

Responses to the change that digitisation represents are many and varied (i.e., a 'mixed bag'), with some companies:

- Focusing their digitisation strategies on specific departments, such as sales and marketing;
- Seeking to embed their digitisation strategy into the company strategy;
- Having multiple digitisation strategies that differ across individual business areas and functions;
- Employing a digitisation strategy only in their IT department.

Given this diversity, it is no surprise that a number of different roles are involved in defining digitisation initiatives, including the CEO, CIO, CFO, Head of Marketing and the HR Director.

Many digitisation efforts result in little more than bolting a digital tool or channel onto an existing or legacy business. And while each digital project may show some success in its own right, delivering tactical results, the strategic reality is that the business needs a reset. Eventually treating every new digital change as just another standalone project generates organisational and technical chaos—chaos that eventually undermines the customer experience resulting in wasted expenditure. Only a comprehensive digital business transformation can create an organisation that flexes to address customers' heightened expectations.

Digital should therefore be looked at holistically with the digital transformation journey commenced through a clearly defined digital vision. Organisations must break down business silos to realise their digital vision. Transforming a company into a digital business is hard and slow and requires significant shifts in organisational thinking and behaviour. Siloed organisations, processes, and systems intensify the operational challenge and prevent the delivery of end-to-end experiences that exceed customer expectations. This is further amplified by different functions competing to own digital.

# 5.11 The Challenges of Going Digital

## A Digital Change Mindshift

> *Taking a digital-first approach is a journey towards a new way of doing business. It requires a mindshift first, followed by technology and process shifts. You can't overhaul your platforms and solutions without changing your culture and thinking. Otherwise that risks replacing legacy infrastructure with modern technology, at great expense, but with little impact on customer and business outcomes (Brett Pitts, Head of Digital, Wells Fargo).*

For digital change to be effective, there must be a fundamental acceptance of the need for change with new ways of thinking, adaptation, etc.

---

### The Six Challenges of Digital Transformation

Recent research highlighted in the Harvard Business Review (2016) has reported that the greatest challenges facing companies going through digital transformation are:

1. Top down structures
2. An inability to experiment
3. Limited change management capabilities
4. Legacy systems
5. A risk averse culture
6. An inability to work across silos.

Other barriers to digitisation include the costs and shortage of skilled staff, all of which will restrict how prepared businesses are to manage the technological changes that are emerging and will emerge over the next decade.

Gill and Fenwick (2015) devised the following seven item questionnaire as part of their research in assessing an organisation's readiness for going digital, with responses measured according to an agreement scale.

### Assessing an Organisation's Readiness to Go Digital

1. Our CEO sets a clear vision for digital in our business
2. We fully understand the potential of digital to change how we create and deliver value to our customers
3. We have the culture to succeed with our digital strategy
4. We have the right people to define our digital strategy
5. We have the necessary technology to execute our digital strategy
6. We have the necessary people and skills to execute our digital strategy
7. We have the necessary processes to execute our digital strategy

The above questions can serve as a basis for broadly assessing an organisation's digital readiness.

## The Challenge of Managing a Two Speed Ambidextrous Organisation

*The ambidextrous organisation: An ability to succeed in both the core current business model and a future model that involves significant innovation.*

In going digital, businesses need to enact a parallel (or two speed) organisation that is dynamic enough to transact today, as well as build for the future. The organisation must operate bimodally in order to cater for all customers in continuing to deliver services in traditional ways. This may mean embracing internal disruption before the external market does the disrupting. Organisations won't achieve their digital aims without their employees going the extra mile while keeping their day job going.

> *Continuing to execute on legacy products and services matters tremendously to the near-term health of a business, but it's just not enough to win in the future. The pace of disruption in a world of 'wicked problems' requires leaders to balance what has worked in the past, with what will be required to win in the future (Reimer, Feuerstein, Meighan & Kelly, 2017).*

The business must be fit to react quickly to whatever the future may throw at it, with adaptable, creative, and capable people. This is a huge change for traditional organisations that have perfected ways of working that deliver efficiently and effectively at scale, with legacy products and services, but don't lend themselves to agility and innovation. It requires agility: the ability to think fast, decide fast, execute fast, fail fast, and scale fast. The organisation must be able to:

- Run planning and execution in parallel; and
- Balance the need to optimise today's business while simultaneously preparing for tomorrow's business.

These are two fundamentally different management challenges. The real problem is doing both simultaneously! It incorporates:

- Exploitation of the existing business model, including products, services, customers, challenges, etc., primarily focused on developing operational efficiencies while responding incrementally to changes required by the market; and
- Exploration of new innovations that may be disruptive of the existing business model.

A too narrower focus on exploitation may jeopardise future survival. A too narrower focus on exploration may expose the organisation to significant risk, with products and services that may not reach commercialisation.

Managing the scope of digital transformation is therefore important in the context of:

1. The risk to Business-As-Usual (BAU) operations
2. The digital readiness of the organisation and its workforce.

## New Competencies and Ways of Working

New competencies required in going digital include:

- A variety of technology specialisations – including cloud, social, mobile, data analytics, data science, machine learning, app development and cognitive computing (refer earlier to Chapter 4.2). This technology competency needs to be combined with strategic partner relationship management, research and development, innovation and strategic thinking.
- Service life-cycle management – customer orientation, business and financial acumen, service design, multi-disciplinary team leadership, stakeholder management.
- Business management – planning, data management, financial modeling, workforce planning, change management, stakeholder management, capability development.

Going digital requires new ways of working, with the adoption of more agile work practices, collaboration, design thinking, and systems thinking. Radical rethinking of procurement, delegations and resource allocation is also required with executive and management strategic priorities and governance having to keep pace with the speed of change.

Effective digital execution is now core to business success.

## 5.12 Approaches to Going Digital

There are various approaches to going digital as referred to earlier including:

- Forming and running a separate innovation team, parallel yet distinct from the existing core business, reporting up to a central leadership team;
- Funding a separate company that becomes an innovation incubator;
- Establishing a digital lab or pod to digitise the new processes;
- Executing in parallel, rolling-in and scaling up (refer to Chapter 6, Step 4).

Integration and collaboration between the core and innovative business streams are vital with functional counterparts interacting directly to exchange ideas and achieve better alignment. That said, there is potential for dysfunction as the skills, mindset and culture that characterise the core business are likely to be different to that required for the innovation team. Productivity and time horizons are also likely to vary between the two groups, challenging perceptions and contributions of the groups. Notwithstanding HR is strategically placed to craft the conditions for a successful ambidextrous operation. There should be clear communication as to how and when the switch over will happen—either a single 'big bang', parallel running for a defined period, or a progressive switch over for specific products following pilots and testing.

Many companies start small, focusing on reshaping one business unit or product line, not wanting to put their existing revenue streams at risk.

Chapter 6

# The Nine Key Steps in Digital Transformation

## 6.1 The Nine Key Steps in Digital Transformation

The following nine key steps involved in addressing a major digital (and business) transformation project have been set out below. These steps are listed in a typical sequence (although some will be occurring in more of a piecemeal or *ad hoc* manner. They are not necessarily exhaustive, and are provided as a guide only. They may vary in scope and scale according to particular organisational requirements and circumstances. They may apply to the organisation as a whole, or part thereof (e.g., a Business Unit)—there are a lot of moving parts! They can also apply in the cases of redesigning the IT operating model to support digital ambitions. For a major transformation the time frame may stretch over two or three years.

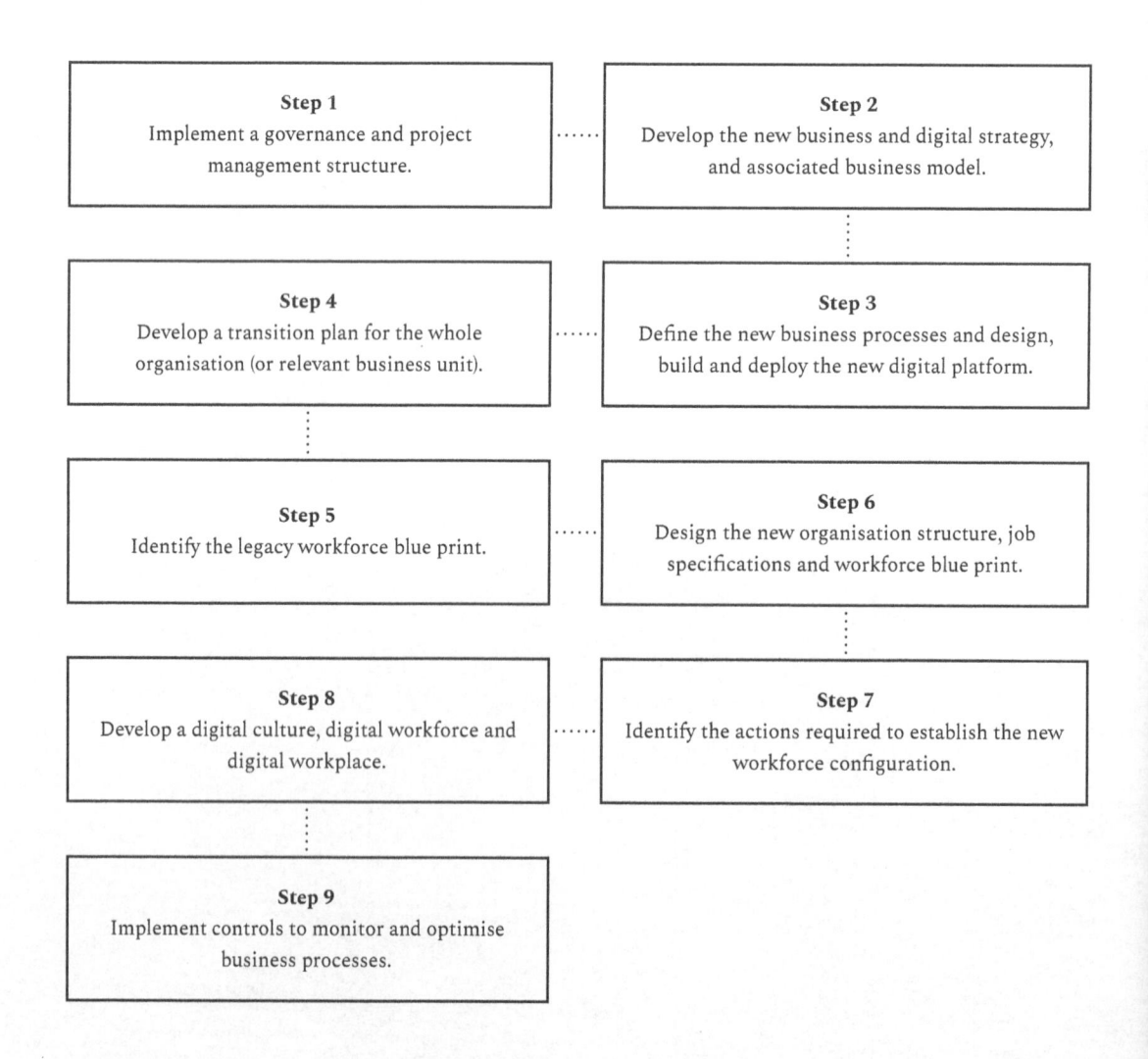

**Step 1**
Implement a governance and project management structure.

**Step 2**
Develop the new business and digital strategy, and associated business model.

**Step 4**
Develop a transition plan for the whole organisation (or relevant business unit).

**Step 3**
Define the new business processes and design, build and deploy the new digital platform.

**Step 5**
Identify the legacy workforce blue print.

**Step 6**
Design the new organisation structure, job specifications and workforce blue print.

**Step 8**
Develop a digital culture, digital workforce and digital workplace.

**Step 7**
Identify the actions required to establish the new workforce configuration.

**Step 9**
Implement controls to monitor and optimise business processes.

These key steps are elaborated upon below, more so for the purposes of providing an outline or overview, rather than a more detailed analysis and prescription. The emphasis is on workforce related matters as opposed to IT matters.

## 6.2 Step 1: Implement a Governance & Project Management Structure

Clarity around governance and decision-making is essential and to that end, the following governance and decision-making structures are recommended.

### The Steering Committee (SC)

The Steering Committee (SC) would have a governance role with a defined charter. Its' composition should be representative of the various core competencies of the organisation, with senior level appointees as members. Some of the main responsibilities of this SC should include:

- Providing an independent and impartial assessment of the business/digital transformation project, including risks;
- Providing assistance and/or advice concerning the project, including the Project Plan and associated resources;
- Monitoring and querying the project progress, activities, outputs and costs to the extent that the project is meeting its targets;
- Regular reporting, including making recommendations, to the Executive Leadership Team and/or CEO.

    *Note.* The SC should be responsible to the Executive Leadership Team and/or CEO.

Reference has been made to a Business and Digital Strategy Investigative Team in Step 2. This Team would report to either the CEO and Executive Leadership Team, or the Steering Committee (SC) if the latter had been initially formed. Once the future direction of the digital transformation has been established, including the associated Enterprise Level Digital Transformation Plan Report and recommendations, this Investigative Team would be disbanded.

## The Project Management Team (PMT)

The Project Management Team (PMT) would be responsible for the overall management of the business/digital transformation project. It would have an operational focus and would most likely include some members who have a full-time involvement in the project.

Typically the PMT should include representatives from Business Strategy, IT and HR, plus the various affected Business Units (e.g., sales, marketing, design, manufacturing, finance, legal). It may include external Subject Matter Experts who would add objectivity and expertise to this Team. Product Managers (refer to Chapter 4) should also be members of the PMT where applicable.

The composition of this PMT may vary during the life of the project, depending upon the stage of progress reached. The PMT would be responsible to the SC.

## Architecture and Infrastructure Review Boards

Some organisations adopt an Architecture and Infrastructure Review Board to oversee the IT development.

## Other Management/Deployment Bodies

Standards for deployment often call for multiple testing groups and management bodies to sign off on code.

## New Transformer in Chief Role (or a Version Thereof)

Depending upon the extent or magnitude of the change, a new Transformer in Chief Role may be created, or a version thereof. Such a role would be charged with coordinating and managing comprehensive changes that address everything from updating how a company works to building entirely new businesses. The role would include understanding market trends and developments in technology and customer behaviour, both inside and outside of the particular industry sector. The Transformer in Chief would be a member of the Business and Digital Strategy Investigative Team and also the SC.

## 6.3 Step 2: Develop the New Proposed Business & Digital Strategy & Associated Business Model

> *Often a strategy is directional to an endpoint that is littered with ambiguity... The journey that companies are embarking upon is different to ever before because it is not just about solution or product, it is also about leading and managing a workforce with different skills (Reimer, Feuerstein, Meighan & Kelly, 2017).*

**Business and Digital Strategy Investigative Team**

Whilst this task is a shared responsibility, and ultimately the responsibility of the CEO and the Board, the key person leading this task would typically be the new Transformer in Chief Role or a Business Strategy Executive.

This Executive should work closely with the CIO (or equivalent) and the HR Director (or equivalent). Other Subject Matter Experts (both from inside and outside of the organisation) may form part of an initial Business and Digital Strategy Investigative Team. This Team would be charged with investigating the feasibility of various new business and digital strategies, and associated new business model(s), and report on the same in the form of an Enterprise Level Digital Plan (see below).

The digital strategy and execution must be clear about what the desired outcome is and how it will benefit customers. Part of this purpose should be a clear vision of the organisation's values, ethics and responsibilities, viz:

- What does the organisation stand for?
- What do its customers expect?
- What are customers' value drivers?
- How will this be reflected in the firm's decisions and practices and its behaviours?

## A Portfolio View

In developing a digital strategy, the first step for a large organisation is to take a portfolio view and consider how digital will disrupt, or is already disrupting, the various Business Units. By assessing each Business Unit individually and then creating an aggregate view, the organisation can assess the significance of digital disruption across its activities and clearly prioritise areas for consideration.

Such priorities should be determined either because a Business Unit is under threat, or because it is positioned to pursue new opportunities. More importantly, consideration can be given to those responses that need to be made at a Business Unit level, and those that will require enterprise wide action.

## The Enterprise Level Digital Transformation Plan

The Enterprise Level Digital Transformation Plan should comprehensively argue the business case for transformation. Issues that typically may form part of this business case, some of which may be specific to various Business Units, include:

- Goals of the transformed business;
- Transition to the cloud provisioning of IT systems;
- Design and development of the new digital platform and associated architecture;
- Reconfiguration of business processes to reduce costs in IT and HR operations;
- Estimate of increased direct sales/revenue to customers, including an enhanced app for smart phones and tablets;
- Estimate of the transformation costs and investment;
- Estimate of the ongoing costs;
- Estimate of cost efficiencies/productivity gains that can be achieved (e.g., resource and time savings);
- Approach to running a two speed or ambidextrous organisation (in the short to medium term), including the risk to BAU operations;
- The new organisational structure and new workforce requirements/configuration in broad terms;
- An evaluation of the impact of changes on assets employed and their fair value;

- Introduction of new services that leverage customer location data;
- Divestment of legacy manufacturing facilities;
- Amendment of risk policies to cater for the digital environment;
- Other benefits that might be generated from digitisation, e.g.:
  - Enhanced customer experience;
  - Reduced risk, downtime (manufacturing);
  - Creation of smart workplaces to boost productivity, efficiency.

Traditional balance sheet and funding structures relevant to the historic business model may no longer apply and forecasting may become more hazardous. It is important that equity and financial stakeholders fully understand the degree and nature of change, and the shape of the profit and loss (P&L) and balance sheet, during and after any digital transformation.

Some of the above issues are further discussed in the following key transformational steps.

## Scale of Digital Transformation Envisaged

Important choices need to be made about how digital the organisation should become and how quickly, taking into account the maturity, fitness or readiness of the business to react quickly to the future. These choices include consideration of:

- Identification of the higher purpose of the organisation and where value is created, which starts with a deep and comprehensive internal assessment including a thorough evaluation of the firm's assets – brands, capital, data, customers, products, people and capability gaps;

  **Note.** As referred to in Chapter 1, the unbundling of current products and services may uncover or present a focus on new core business.

- Identification of the *status quo* of the current digital environment, including the technologies that are currently being used;
- Assessment of the legacy workforce and systems, and their level of fitness or readiness for transformation;

- The level of disruption that is acceptable, and to which parts of the business;
- The risk to BAU operations.

*Note.* *Refer to Chapter 5 on Phases of Transformation that includes: (1) products, (2) channels and (3) operations, ranging in scale from enhancement to transformation.*

A compelling narrative should be developed as part of the Enterprise Level Digital Transformation Plan including:

- The need to change (i.e., business survival) and the benefits that can expect to follow;
- The ways and extent to which digital innovation may impact on the organisation, including both threats and opportunities;
- How the business plans to respond, both at a Business Unit level and at a wider enterprise level.

Additionally this Plan should also include reference to the following:

- A redefinition or confirmation of the vision, mission, and values;
- A redefinition or confirmation of the organisational critical capability(s) and core competencies;

*Note.* *As referred to previously in Chapter 4.7 and 4.8, ultimately an organisation is about capabilities and competencies that deliver value in the form of products and services (i.e., what the organisation is good at).*

- The business case for digital transformation as referred to the various items listed above;
- The new business model and digital strategy, including the scale of digital disruption envisaged and timing;
- The approach to digitisation (e.g., establishing a Centre of Excellence, Digital Labs, establishing a separate organisation running in parallel, rolling-in and scaling up);
- Identification of key measures for success;
- A Transition Plan outline (refer also Step 4) including associated resourcing issues with indicative time lines;

- Creation of a digital culture, digital workplace and digital workforce;
- Confirmation of governance and management structures for the transformation project;
- Next steps.

This Enterprise Level Digital Transformation Plan would then be considered and endorsed (or otherwise) at Executive Level and ultimately by the Board. Unless digital transformation is driven from the top, it won't succeed. Effective leaders must communicate a clear vision and commit wholeheartedly, investing in resources, including time and funds.

*Note.* One of the main responsibilities of a Board is to set and/or approve of the strategy of the organisation.

## 6.4 Step 3: Define the New Processes & Design, Build & Deploy the New Digital Platform & Infrastructure

This Step commences with an assessment of existing processes and systems. Then the new processes need to be defined that deliver the desired value to the customer. These run:

- Horizontally across departments and functions and should reflect the supply chain; and
- Vertically to reflect limits of authority, management control and governance.

The new organisation structure (refer Step 6) should be designed to maximise collaboration and integrate process activities across structure boundaries. Particular attention should be paid to process handoffs at internal company and external structural boundaries.

The new digital platform and infrastructure then needs to be designed, developed and then deployed and tested. Architectural planning is important to ensure the systems, offerings, products, interactions and capabilities are appropriate.

## 6.5 Step 4: Develop a Transition or Change Plan

Then a detailed Transition or Change Plan would need to be developed for the project. This should include key tasks, resources and timelines, including a phasing out of the old and a phasing in of the new. More specifically, this Transition Plan, from a workforce perspective, should address the following:

- Integration and coordination complexity;
- The change strategy, various stages of the change, and key responsibilities (refer to Step 8);
- Ramping up the new in terms of workforce capability, including redeployment, retraining, and recruitment, and ramping down the old, including any redundancies (refer to Step 7);
- Beta testing of the new system deployment and running parallel (workforce) systems (where appropriate), or adopting a 'Roll-in' approach (see below);

*Note. Legacy processes that become redundant as a result of the new journey should still be run in parallel until the new journey is fully operational.*

- Education and training of the workforce generally, including creating a digital culture (refer to Step 8);
- Communications to stakeholders including employees in particular (ongoing);

*Note. Genuine digital transformation will affect many people who have no ability to influence the outcome.*

- Appointment of change agents within the business (some of whom will be part-time in addition to their normal duties).

*Note. The appointment of change agents will develop the organisation's change management capability both for the present and the future.*

The skill set required for such a transformation extends beyond being digitally savvy. The key to overcoming internal resistance is helping stakeholders understand how digital transformation will work and how roles will change for the better. Painful surgeries may be needed for survival to ensure the long-term sustainability of the organisation.

**'Rolling-in' Approach**

Roll-in is often a useful option for building scale. Once the rough shape and size of the new digital business is determined through the early stages of testing with a small team, people are gradually added until the team has the capacity to do all of the required work. It may mean starting off with a small portion of current demand and then evolving the new business as work volumes rise (i.e.. a process of scaling and adoption).

## 6.6 Step 5: Identify the Legacy Workforce Blueprint

The steps to configuring and securing the right workforce are to:

- Firstly understand the capabilities, traits, drivers, experience and knowledge that the organisation has now (i.e., the legacy workforce); and
- Secondly determine what will be required in the future.

Then the pipeline to the future workforce can be developed.

Identifying this legacy workforce blueprint (including HR policies and practices and reporting), provides a comprehensive picture of the current workforce make-up including:

- Workforce (role) segmentation and sub-segmentation, including critical roles, 'make' roles, 'buy' roles;
- Demographics (including age, gender);
- Skills profiles;
- Job levels/grades/types;
- Tenure (experience), both with the organisation and in the job;

- Engagement levels;
- Turnover;
- Compensation;
- Performance measures;
- Current investments in training and development;
- List of current HR policies and practices;
- Status of HR data reporting and analytics.

Examining this legacy workforce will identify issues such as:

- Identifying the critical roles and succession planning status;
- Whether HR policies and practices are consistent with the above role segmentation including optimising the ROI in people in those various roles;
- Whether existing outsourcing arrangements are consistent with the business strategy;
- Assessing workforce risks;
- Managing an aging workforce;
- Lowering disruptive turnover;
- Increasing gender diversity, etc.

In this examination, there is a need to adopt a Business-By-Business Unit or portfolio approach (i.e., need a more granular level detail), as workforce behaviours and characteristics can vary dramatically within an organisation.

Furthermore a workforce does not behave in a linear fashion. It flows as people are promoted, leave, transferred, retire, take sabbaticals, etc. Hence it is important to understand the 'liquid workforce': how the workforce is continually changing. It will also show how the workforce will evolve without any intervention so organisations can build a clear picture of what their workforce will look like at a specific date in future (e.g., 3 years, 5 years) including:

- How many skilled people they will have, in what roles and at what level, and how they will leave the workforce, either through retirement or attrition;
- A more granular level of detail on important demographics;

- Where the risks are of loosing people filling critical roles;
- Uncovering opportunities to refocus the people spend.

*Note.* The same legacy workforce approach was adopted by Vie (2016) from AXXA Insurance (120,000 employees and over 100 Business Units) in their major digital strategic workforce transformation project.

The legacy workforce blue print can then be mapped by workforce segment and sub-segments. It sets the stage for calculating the gap with the number and type of employees required in the future. This mapping also forms an essential part of the development of a Strategic Workforce Plan (refer to Part 2 of this book).

*Note.* This is where the AWS Skills-Based Workforce Segmentation Model and the SSQ (refer Appendix D) becomes a vital tool in determining:

- *What are the Critical Roles?*
- *What roles are 'Make' roles?*
- *What roles are 'Buy' roles?*
- *What roles are Specialist' roles?*
- *What is the cost of turnover for these various roles?*
- *What is the level of engagement and retention risk for those roles?*
- *What is the status of succession planning for Critical Roles?*
- *Are current HR policies and practices consistent with the segmentation of roles?*
- *Is the level of investment in people/roles consistent with the segmentation of those roles?*

## 6.7 Step 6: Design the New Organisational Structure

Reference has been made earlier in Chapter 4 to the impact of digital transformation on organisational design. The new structure will need to reflect changes to the operating model and processes, and optimise the organisation's ability to execute its strategy. It should start with and reflect the capabilities and competencies that deliver value in the form of products and services, which is what the organisation is good at.

Structure and roles must be fluid enough to allow and sustain 'digital'. For specific projects, multidisciplinary teams should be brought together from across the organisation that have shared objectives and metrics to deliver on. For such projects, the traditional hierarchies and command and control approaches do not support a connected business. Ideas and inputs may come from various stakeholders with active collaboration fostered with clients, partners and even competitors.

## Future Workforce Considerations

With the development of the new organisation design, many aspects of the business may change including reporting lines and key metrics. New job roles and associated job descriptions (including their skills, experience and qualification requirements), and teams with the right combination of complementary capabilities, can then be formulated. This should occur through a series of Business Unit workshops facilitated by HR.

The shift to digital intelligence requires new roles and skills, as well as new mental models and ways of operating. One of the biggest challenges is to balance the needs and motivations of the legacy workforce versus new employees who bring digital capability. For example, it is important to establish (or enhance) a data science practice. A dedicated group of data scientists allows a firm to go into more depth, and ask more complex questions.

> *Note.* Data scientist and actuaries have broad similarities focusing on deeply on analyzing data. Data science includes two broad sets of skills:

1. Quantitative: mathematics and statistics including the ability to build mathematical and statistical models of organisational processes.
2. Computer science: managing data bases and programming, being data experts who can extract data from multiple sources/systems and shape it into a structure suited for analysis.

The new workforce blueprint should include the following analysis by workforce segment:

- The numbers of roles and employees for each of those roles that remain relatively unchanged;
- The numbers of new digital roles and associated numbers of employees per role (cybersecurity experts, digital marketing specialists, customer experience specialists, computer scientists and IT professionals experienced in cloud-based technologies);
- The numbers of new non-digital roles and associated numbers of employees roles.

This new blueprint should also include reference to the numbers of roles and associated employees that will become redundant. An assessment can then be made regarding which of these roles and employees may be suitable for redeployment, including any associated training.

*Note.* This is where the AWS Skills-Based Workforce Segmentation Model and the SSQ again becomes a vital tool in relation to the above in determining:

- *What are the new Critical Roles?*
- *What roles should remain in-house (i.e., 'make' roles)?*
- *What roles are 'buy' roles?*
- *What roles will need substantial investment in training and development (e.g., Specialist roles)?*
- *What roles should or could be potentially outsourced?*

Skills are like currency, prone to obsolescence. The ideal workforce model for the digital economy is a fluid, blended, and agile portfolio of skillsets. Primary digital skills must be complemented with agile, business-savvy employees with the acumen to drive change. Furthermore, the more customer centric an organisation becomes, the more diverse its workforce will need to become. The future workforce needs to reflect the diversity of customers, including multi-generational engagement across multiple channels.

## Assessing the Value to Labour Cost Ratio of the New Workforce

For the new workforce configuration, structure, and numbers, there should be a general shift towards higher value and higher uniqueness roles (see diagram below). With digital transformation, it is most likely that changes to the Doer segment in the AWS Skills-

Based Workforce Segmentation Model (refer to Appendix D) will result in reduced numbers of staff. The overall impact should be to increase the Value to Labour Cost Ratio of the workforce (compared to the legacy workforce), thus resulting in greater workforce efficiency, effectiveness and sustainability.

Whilst any labour cost reduction can easily be calculated, it is both the value as well as the cost that should be considered. For example, if the Value to Labour Cost Ratio increases as well as the total labour cost decreasing, this would indicate a more capable and efficient workforce that should deliver superior outcomes.

This Value to Labour Cost Ratio can be assessed taking into account the numbers of various roles and their scores and plots according to the SSQ. Comparisons can then be made between the legacy and proposed new workforce to determine the extent of the change. Thus the SSQ offers a unique means of measuring and quantifying this difference.

## General Shift Towards Higher Value and Higher Uniqueness Roles

**Skills Workforce Segmentation Plots**

# 6.8 Step 7: Identify the Required Actions to Establish the New Workforce Configuration

Once the new workforce blue print is developed, it can be overlaid on the legacy workforce blueprint. This overlay would be compared on a role-segment and sub-segment basis, including numbers of roles and people in those roles. For example the number of sales, administration, and customer support roles (i.e., Doer roles) and associated skills and experience requirements for the legacy workforce could be compared with the equivalent new workforce roles. Obviously there are likely to be new roles in the new workforce configuration that do not exist in the legacy workforce as referred to previously (e.g., data scientists and analysts, cybersecurity specialists, customer experience specialists, digital marketing specialists, computer scientists and IT professionals experienced in cloud-based technologies).

Then gaps (including numbers, skills, experience, etc.) and overlaps or surpluses can be determined and decisions made about the transition to the new workforce configuration. Workforce demand and supply can be manipulated using the following workforce leavers. An integrated strategy that focuses on talent identification, recruitment, learning and development and retention, as well as employee engagement, provides the right foundation for transformation.

**Workforce Business and HR Levers**

Workforce demand can be reduced through these levers:

- Outsourcing;
- Automating work through technology;
- Standardising work to make it more efficient;
- Cross-skilling part of the workforce including redeployment;
- Managing performance more effectively;
- Internal promotions;
- Retention;
- Shifting to a different business model.

Workforce demand can be increased (if necessary) by:

- Voluntary turnover;
- Involuntary turnover;
- Retirements.

Workforce supply can be increased through HR levers:

- Recruiting new skills.

## Finance Modelling

The host of HR issues to be considered, with associated finance modelling and costings, include:

- Redeployment options;
- Training;
- Recruitment options;
- Redundancy options.

With various roles segmented according to the AWS Skills-Based Model, this provides a framework for a more fine grained approach to calculating the above costs. Short-term additional HR resources will most likely be required with respect to developing and implementing policies and practices relating to the above, including change management capability (refer to Step 8).

## Workforce Configuration

As Korn Ferry (2016) contend, the ultimate aim is the development and configuration of a workforce that meets the following five criteria:

1. Right shape: right workforce composition, enabling vs. operational, in-sourcing vs. outsourcing, staff vs. management, across the organisation

2. Right site: availability of capable staff at the right locations
3. Right skills: clarity regarding capabilities to meet future goals and actual gaps
4. Right size: required number of staff for the jobs that are needed to achieve the strategic goals efficiently and effectively
5. Right spend: right cost/investment to the business in achieving the above.

## 6.9 Step 8: Develop a Digital Culture, Digital Workforce & Digital Workplace

As referred to in Chapter 5, people are at the heart of the digital economy—their primacy remains with the human factors arguably the most important element in making a digital transformation useful, successful, and valuable. Technology and processes alone might enable but will neither differentiate nor make change stick. There are differences between engaging in digital and becoming a digital organisation. Success today requires a shift from technology and processes as the primary enabler of change, to encompass the significantly broader and deeper people impact associated with digital transformation.

The transformation of the traditional workplace environment to incorporate new technologies, real estate, people management practices (including learning, leadership, engagement), have been dealt with in Chapters 4 and 8. Chapter 2 has dealt with innovation. Chapter 7 has dealt with the extended role of the HR Director/Manager in leading and creating a digital culture, workplace and workforce.

Reference has been made earlier in Step 4 for the need of change agents in the Transition Plan. Essentially this Step 8 is about Change Management, an overview of which is outlined below including various change models.

## About Change Management

*Change definition: a transformation or transition from one state or condition to another.*

Change Management is about shifting mindsets and behaviours. In any major transition, firstly a Change Strategy needs to be developed followed by the development of a Change Plan or a Transition Plan as the case may be.

## Change Models

There are various models of change including the following:

- Lewin's Unfreeze-Change-Freeze Model (1947) that involves unfreezing, change and refreezing involving letting go of the old and establishing new patterns over time).

- Dunphy and Stace's Contingency Model (1990) that constitutes a contingency approach to change taking into account environmental factors and leadership capabilities as crucial in any change, but omits consideration of organisational factors.

- Kotter's 8-Step Model of Change (1995) that involves creating a climate for change, engaging and enabling the organisation, and implementing and sustaining for change. This model assumes that change is a one-off with a positive, stable end, with an emphasis on change leaders without asking for buy-in from others and can be seen as linear.

- Hardy's S-Curve of Change (1995) that is based on the organisational life cycle and intersection of the sigmoid curves for change.

- Prosci ADKAR Model (2003), with a focus on people, based on what individuals need for change then scaled up to apply to organisations. This model comprises five elements of (1) awareness of the need for change, (2) desire to support change, (3) knowledge of how to change, (4) ability to demonstrate new skills and behaviour, and (5) reinforcement to make the change stick.

Each of these models have their own strengths and weaknesses, with all lacking empirical evidence. A more detailed analysis of these models is beyond the scope of this book.

Notwithstanding the above, planning and managing change involves five key stages:

1. Determining the need for change: triggered by on-going business analysis, changes to external conditions, identification of new opportunities, etc.

2. Developing a case for change: including options, likely achievements, impacts, risks and resource implications, costs and benefits, timescale, and including what may happen if change doesn't occur.

3. Communicating the vision for change: presenting a compelling narrative that sets out how the new situation will be better.

4. Developing a strategy and plan for change: having clear project management procedures, clear accountability, objectives and timelines.

    *Note.* *This could include a Training Needs Analysis (TNA) to identify the training needs associated with the change.*

5. Managing the change process: seeking tangible benefits and embedding new systems, processes and cultures into every day activity.

## Phases of Change for Employees

With respect to employees, the vision and communication for change includes the following progressive phases of realisation in their ascending order of importance:

- Contact;
- Awareness;
- Understanding;
- Engagement;
- Acceptance;
- Commitment;
- Internalisation.

## Key Accountabilities for Change

The Change or Transition Plan should define key accountabilities and working arrangements including various roles such as:

- Sponsor;
- Project Manager;
- Key user/stakeholder representatives;
- Communications lead;
- Specialists.

## Three Axes of Transformational Change

Dichter, Gagnon and Alexander (1993) identify three axes of transformational change:

1. Top-down direction: to create focus throughout an organisation and develop conditions for performance improvement – to get people at all levels to take a fresh approach to solving problems and improving performance.
2. Broad-based bottom-up performance improvement.
3. Cross-functional core process redesign: to link activities, functions, and information in new ways to achieve breakthrough improvements in cost, quality and timeliness.

Each axis is necessary. If top-down initiatives are lacking or faulty, managers will be left to guess where to aim new skills or activities. If bottom-up involvement is absent, motivation will falter, momentum will flag, opportunities for improvement will be overlooked, and new skills and behaviour will not be built. If horizontal core processes are ignored, function-specific efforts will never add up to the critical mass of change required. The result may be an *ad hoc* collection of initiatives that can sap rather than build energy.

Putting too much weight on top-down efforts risks creating cynicism and confusion; excessive emphasis on bottom-up efforts means people may focus on issues that will not make any difference competitively; and bias towards cross-functional processes could produce a solution so complex in design that implementing it is beyond an organisation's capabilities.

> All companies, whether they recognise it or not, have a few (three to five) core processes or functions that deliver the majority of an enterprise's value to its customers. For example, in the widget business, the core functions would be designing, manufacturing and marketing and selling widgets.

Organisations need to embed this ability to change into their DNA so that they can continually respond and become digitally sustainable.

## 6.10 Step 9: Implement Controls to Monitor & Optimise Business Processes & Outcomes

Controls need to be implemented with appropriate reporting to monitor and optimise business processes and business outcomes. Performance should be compared against KPIs and also against the key factors for success identified in Step 2. Typically this would include, amongst other things, measures around customer experience and the financial impact of the digital strategy and associated investments. It is also vital for businesses to track and benchmark their digital transformation to ensure they remain competitive within their industry.

Chapter 7

# Two Key Extended Roles in Digital Transformation

## 7.1  Two Key Extended Roles

As foreshadowed earlier, digital transformation involves the blending of two key disciplines: IT and HR. As such, both the CIO and the HR Director/Manager have key and extended roles to play in a digital transformation project. With the intersection of these two disciplines, both of these roles sit in 'the eye of the storm'. These previous back-office operations now need to take centre stage. It is essential that a productive partnership be formed between the two, with cross-functional collaboration required to successfully navigate the transformation, and to promote the development of digital skills and culture. The two extended roles of the CIO and the HR Director/Manager (or the equivalent of these two roles) are elaborated upon below.

## 7.2  The Role of the CIO

### The Two Hats of the CIO

For the CIO, the digital economy represents an opportunity to take a frontline leadership role in transforming the business and becoming a standard bearer for driving corporate performance through digitisation. CIOs will be at the vanguard of achieving the coalescence of business and technology strategies. Given the massive scope of change that digitisation demands, the challenge is fundamentally one of enterprise leadership. CIOs need to wear two hats:

1. An IT leadership hat
2. An enterprise leadership hat

   In so doing, CIOs need to:

- Frame a productive dialogue about the business potential, goals and structure of digitisation in their organisations;
- Play a critical role in setting realisable goals and creating the roadmap that will direct the organisation to its' digital destination;

- Identify business opportunities and define strategies for realising those opportunities, while also identifying and managing risks.

The above requires a change in focus for the CIO, but also for other members of the executive team who might not normally consider strategic links with the CIO as essential. The expanded and influential role of the CIO will also be reflected in deeper external relationships and cross-functional networks. Digital transformation is a test of the IT department's ability to collaborate.

## Chief Digital Officer: A Fragmented Approach to Digitisation Transformation?

Responses to the need for digitisation transformation can be haphazard. Some organisations introduce the new position of Chief Digital Officer (CDO). However adding another chief to the already crowded C-suite is often unnecessary and potentially counter-productive. Appointing a CDO as the company's 'digital *el supremo*' effectively makes digitisation a silo, whereas the key to successfully transforming an organisation for the digital economy is to ensure that digitisation is a whole-of-organisation undertaking.

The potential appointment of a CDO constitutes an organisational contradiction with such a fragmented approach to digitisation. It risks inconsistent strategies and stymies the agility required to remain competitive against new market entrants and shifting economic trends.

The most qualified and best placed person to take on the role of the digital '*el supremo*' is the CIO, who understands enterprise strategy and is already well positioned to navigate internal and external stakeholder relationships to cultivate digitisation. There is clear opportunity for the CIO, in a fast changing competitive and technology landscape, to provide the leadership and insight that will ensure a more robust embrace of digitisation. The ultimate challenge is to turn that opportunity into reality.

## 7.3 The Role of the HR Director/Manager

**The Evolution of the Role of HR**

HRs' journey of reinvention has extended over the past few decades. It has progressively remodelled itself, of necessity, in name, function and its relationship with business, in an upward spiral of strategic importance to its stakeholders. Previously business leaders have viewed HR as an addendum to the real business. It has been viewed as an ancillary function (i.e., a passive support function that delivered employee services) and not a core one, being kept outside and alongside the business.

The focus of HR has now shifted away from the traditional role of representing the employees, to one of utilising the organisation's human capital to assist management in achieving its' objectives and driving business success. HR now needs to be seen as performing as a valuable business contributor at worst, and a vital or essential strategic function/activity at best, extending well beyond the HR archetype of the past.

> *HRs' role is fundamentally about executing the organisation's strategy through the workforce. It's about building the people and the organisational capability to deliver on the business strategy. HRs' focus should be on bringing value to the business though effective workforce strategies aligned with the business strategy. This could include helping the business succeed be it in innovation, customer service, cost reduction, competitiveness, growth, etc.*

**HR Managing with Ambiguous Authority**

Notwithstanding the reconceptualisation of the role of HR, it has been a much maligned profession, typically lacking in strategic insight and under resourced. Some HR professionals are overwhelmed by the scale of change needed to address or respond to in a highly competitive market. Furthermore HR Departments are typically under resourced. Business disruption puts HR skills to the test, including managerial skills, risk taking, and how the entire human capital of the organisation is lead during challenging times.

It should be noted that CEOs and other operating executives are rarely experts on people management and workplace issues—they often have no relevant experience. Many leaders of today are drawn from a financial background whose model of governance is focused on maximising shareholder value, with less emphasis on the interests of employees. Some only have a cursory understanding of the strategic management of human capital—their most important intangible asset—and contemporary people management practices.

A challenge for HR is trying to influence managers to adopt effective human capital or workforce strategies and follow procedures and practices without having direct power over them. This is termed 'managing with ambiguous authority'. HR therefore has to rely on personal power and influence, and to that end, strong relationship building skills and internal consulting skills are an essential attribute.

HR needs mastery over 'hard' skills (e.g., business acumen, digital intelligence), and harder skills (previously known as 'soft' skills (e.g., including communication, behaviour, leadership, emotional intelligence, cultural intelligence, professional ethics).

## HRs' Role in Digital Transformation

As referred to above, HR is undergoing rapid and profound change. It is now being asked to help lead the digital transformation in these three areas:

- Digital workforce: How can organisations drive new management practices, a culture of innovation and sharing, and a set of talent practices that facilitate a new network-based organisation?

- Digital workplace: How can organisations design a working environment that enables productivity, uses modern communication tools and promotes engagement, wellness, and a sense of purpose?

- Digital HR: How can organisations change the HR function itself to operate in a digital way, use digital tools and apps to deliver solutions, and continuously experiment and innovate?

HRs' role transformation is as inevitable as the transformation happening in the business world. HR is effectively now the business—not a partner to the business. It is undergoing a dramatic shift from transactional excellence to becoming an architect of digital transformation. More than ever before, the corporate strategy for large companies hinges on their people strategy. The future role for HR is a value creating, integrated component of the business.

One of the challenges for HR is guiding the migration of the workforce into the new era, galvanising the workforce of the future. It should be instrumental in facilitating the transformation of the workforce to align it with the digital needs of the business. It must help management and employees rapidly transform and adapt to the digital way of thinking.

HR must therefore join the conversation about digitalising the business. It has a key leadership and pivotal role to play in the reconfiguration of the workforce and the associated transition. It must reorient itself focusing people on the changing human capital issues their companies face. This means going beyond digitising HR platforms to developing digital workplaces and digital workforces, and to deploying technology that changes how people work and the way they relate to each other at work. Refer to Chapter 8 for further analysis and discussion on these challenges.

Fortunately the path to digital HR is becoming clearer, with expanded options, new platforms, and a wide variety of tools to build the twenty-first-century digital organisation, workforce, and workplace. The entire marketplace is shifting from tools that automate traditional HR practices to platforms and apps that make life at work better.

Ulrich (2017) also contends that there is a new external focus of HR—how it delivers value to customers, investors, and communities outside of the organisation, as much as employees and line management inside. He contends that there is a shift to which HR practices have business impacts where HR drives customer share and investor confidence.

## HRs' New Skills Requirement

To embrace its new extended role, HR should have know how in the following areas:

- A sound understanding of the business, the business strategy and business acumen, and strategic skills to align HR policies and practices with the business strategy, connecting workforce decisions to business outcomes;
- Knowledge around how digital changes the fabric of communication, including the whole dynamic with customers;
- A deep knowledge about workforce and workplace issues, including the various areas of HR specialisation (e.g., culture, remuneration and benefits, engagement and retention, recruitment and selection, organisational design, organisational development, change management, learning and development, leadership development, etc.);
- Some information technology 'smarts' (although not excessively so), including the development of a digital workforce strategy and the know how to use digital tools that pervade the employment landscape;

- Marketing in promoting the employment brand and social media capabilities;
- HR analytics in the use of data to forecast needs, and an understanding the drivers, systems and capabilities, providing executives with workforce insights and helping them to act on the same;
- Organisational development and change management capabilities;
- Internal consulting skills and development of effective business partnerships.

HR Directors/Managers should think like economists – good at making sense of markets, experts in collecting data and analysing it, and developing forecasts on business cycles and employment levels. Additionally they need a sixth sense about what is right and wrong when it comes to decision-making about people.

## HRs' Extended New Role

Building on the above skill set, and more specifically, HRs' extended role should also include the following tasks:

- Developing management's capacity to address people management issues;
- Managing the HR capability and resources, including how the mix of HR staff may change from generalists to specialists (e.g., data scientists, statisticians);

    *Note.* *The HR operating model should be in synchronicity with the business model, including HR resources and capabilities in a changing mix. Where the business is decentralized, then so should be the HR Department. Where the business is centralized, then the HR Department should also be so centralised.*

- Developing digital capabilities and selection of mobile apps with a focus on productivity, engagement, teamwork and career growth, and on enablement to help people get work done in more effective and productive ways;

    *Note.* *The new priorities for HR fitting under the digital umbrella include: cloud connectivity, real-time operations, design thinking, simplicity, embedded analytics and mobile first.*

- Building an integrated employee experience platform, including taking self-service to new heights through online HR and knowledge portals, help desk support, live chat, and case management tools.

This multi-disciplinary skill set may require a new breed of HR professionals. Today's business environment is more complex than ever before, creating an unmatched opportunity for HR to create value for the business.

---

### The Concept of the 'T' Manager and the HR Director/Manager

The concept of the 'T' Manager is a manager with deep meaningful subject matter knowledge in one field (the vertical stem of the T), and a broad understanding across other areas (the horizontal arm of the T). Thus this type of manager incorporates deep subject matter expertise, combined with broader skills and knowledge, particularly 'soft' skills, including relationship building, etc.

Applied to the HR Director or Manager:

- The horizontal arm of the T should include strategic thinking, business acumen, and internal consulting skills;
- The vertical stem of the T should include deep knowledge of the workforce, people management and HR analytics.

---

## Arguments for the Preservation of the HR Function and Profession

Cariss and Vorhauser (2017) in their book titled *Cliffhanger*, contend that HR is potentially on the brink of extinction due to their ineffectiveness in recent times, and a questionable capability to meet the challenges of the digital workplace. Whether these concerns are due solely to HR is debatable, as referred to earlier, many Boards, CEOs and Executives are somewhat ignorant of the importance of the people factor. They have not necessarily recognised the importance of this factor to business success (or otherwise paid lip service to it), and the potential role that HR can play, including their desired capabilities.

Arguments put forward for the retention of the HR function by Cariss and Vorhauser (2017) include the following:

> **The Arguments for Retaining HR (Cariss and Vorhauser, 2017)**
>
> - A strategic focus:
>   - Human capital is a strategic organisational asset, and the most expensive one;
>   - Alignment of human capital with the business requires strategic oversight and cross-functional integration;
>   - Only HR has oversight and understanding of the organisation's human capital base that otherwise risks becoming fragmented in HRs' absence.
> - Business performance:
>   - Human capital is the largest predictor of organisational performance.
> - Human experience:
>   - Increased digital automation reduces HRs' need to be involved in people processes, but heightens the need for creating an engaging and authentic workforce experience;
>   - As culture and talent underpin innovation, HR plays a crucial role in creating an environment that promotes and accelerates creative and divergent thinking.

- Expertise:
  - HR is a field of expertise and professional domain that requires Subject Matter Expertise;
  - HR constitutes a balancing act between the diverse personal and professional needs and aspirations of people, and the vision and mission of the organisation.

- Business Support:
  - People are high maintenance assets compared with machines;
  - An effective centralised HR support unit minimises business distractions;
- HR provides an objective voice in the event of employee disputes and workplace issues.

Cariss and Vorhauser argue quite correctly that HR is both a driver and a passenger in this reinvention scenario. It is instrumental in transitioning organisational structure and culture to position the business for success.

Chapter 8

# Developing a Digital Workplace Strategy

## 8.1 Communications Are Critical in the Digital Economy

The digital economy requires people to collaborate, solve problems, and think creatively to meet customer expectations. Workplaces are being re-invented to become less structured, more diverse, more interactive, and engaging. Work that was once performed on wired connections is steadily migrating to wireless. Communications networks are becoming more critical infrastructure that underpin fast information flows and accelerates innovation. For contract workers, being able to connect with and continuously engage with these cohorts will be essential to success. Agile organisations are connected organisations. Connected businesses create ecosystems made up of networks of people from within and outside of the organisation (refer earlier to Chapter 1).

As the workplace becomes more fragmented and less routine, it's critical to look to technology to bring people together with a purpose. The digital workplace therefore is all about facilitating employees' ability to do their job by collaborating, communicating and connecting with others. It's about enabling them to utilise technology to access data and collaborate with one another at any time and on any device. This constitutes a vital element of developing a digital culture. The goal is to forge productive relationships within and beyond natural work groups, and to enable knowledge sharing across the organisation. To that end, organisations need to develop an effective digital workplace strategy.

The flexibility promised by digital transformation has mobile at its core. Mobile adoption is pervasive and growing—the future is on-demand and mobile giving people access to corporate applications, customers and data. However mobile technology is a double-edged sword. It allows access, flexibility, and collaboration, but also potentially results in a loss of control, and exposes organisation to privacy and network security risks, particularly with the changing cybersecurity landscape.

> **Note.** *It has often been stated that the greatest point of vulnerability of an organisation's data is the behaviour and lack of mindfulness of employees.*

## 8.2 HR Technology in the Digital Workplace

There is a need to incorporate a HR technology strategy into the business strategy mix. The digital workplace environment encompasses all the technologies people use to get work done in today's workplace. These technologies should complement the organisation's core ERP/HRMS infrastructure and be standardised and integrated in a way that:

- Support changes in working styles;
- Unify offline and online communications (by keeping employees connected through their mobile devices);
- Focus on employees' experience;
- Support virtual work environments.

The traditional workplace was born before the intranet so it's not wired for it. Many companies are adopting digital workplace strategies as a way of retrofitting modern tools and technology into their current infrastructure.

### Eight Key Functions in the Digital Workplace

The digital workplace should accommodate these eight functions and activities, with their associated technologies and equipment:

1. Messaging: provides a fast way to communicate with colleagues (email, instant messaging, mobile messaging)
2. Productivity: enables knowledge workers to get their jobs done efficiently (word processes, spread sheet software, presentation software, calculator)
3. Collaboration: enables employees to work with each other and with partners (communities, web conferencing)
4. Communication: supports information sharing and internal publishing (portals/intranet, blogs, personalised home page)
5. Business applications: enables employees to access self-service applications online (expense claims, HR systems, CRM, ERP)

6. Crowd sourcing: enables organisations to gather ideas, inputs and thoughts from employees (ideation platform, polling, survey, forums)
7. Connectivity: helps locate experts and colleagues across the organisation (employee directory, organisation chart, rich profiles)
8. Mobility: enables access of tools away from the physical office or workplace (PC/laptop, mobile/smart phone, home office, remote scanners).

*Note. Enterprise social networking has seen explosive growth. Blogs, social networking and video sharing are the most popular features.*

Overall, this HR technology in the digital workplace serves the following four main purposes:

1. Streamlines administration work
2. Innovatse HR practices
3. Provides access to information
4. Creates social experiences and connectivity.

## BYOA (Bring Your Own App)

More and more people are opting to use their personal productivity applications like Google Docs and Dropbox to collaborate at work. These apps don't require involvement from IT and are fast and familiar. It's important to opt for tools that can work together and support integration.

## Digital HR Self-Service Operations

*Digital HR at its simplest means eliminating paper forms and publications, and moving to electronic documents and online information exchange, on a par with consumer online experience.*

Human Capital Management ecosystems are being expanded to include automated task management and communications optimisation. Employee self-service includes access to information and transaction completion incorporating tools that can track help requests, help desk resolutions, interactive employee exchanges, etc. Routine tasks can be afforded onto employees with self-service administration options. The potential benefits include:

- Improved employee experience;
- More efficiently creating and tracking appropriate information;
- Gaining additional data about the use, clarity and relevance of that information;
- Generating statistics on the efficiency and effectiveness of overall HR operations.

## The Effective Use of Technology

Any new technology should provide clarity about who should use it, how they should use it, and to support whatever the objectives. Introducing an abundance of technology options with no focus on how they empower the workforce can be overwhelming and ineffective. There are a multitude of technologies over the employee life cycle to source, select, engage, and develop.

The effective use of technology in the digital workplace must therefore be underpinned by appropriate controls, which means appropriate governance and management processes must be in place. Information flow and use must also comply with the organisation's policies and industry regulations. Employees require policy training on the type of information they should and should not share in the digital workplace, including how to handle personal data. They also need to be equipped with genuinely transformative new digital skills that:

- Gives them the ability to adapt;
- Provides them with the most relevant tools and platforms;
- Conveys new motivations; and
- Fosters the know-how to re-imagine their knowledge work in new ways that are much more adaptable, rich, scalable and resilient.

Organisations also need to build a digital employment brand. Everything an organisation does in the digital and socially networked world affects candidates' decision to work there. Messaging across sites and experiences should be monitored and controlled.

Chapter 9

# Technology & HR Analytics

## 9.1 HR Analytics Now a Business Discipline

HR or workforce analytics is the process of discovering, interpreting and communicating meaningful patterns in workforce-related data to inform decision making and improve performance. These analytics have both management and predictive applications giving business leaders the insight to improve people decision making. Furthermore, these analytics are not only about data analysis but also about change management—generating meaningful insights to drive behaviour change and increase organisational effectiveness.

HR analytics is undergoing a seismic shift. Driven by the widespread adoption of cloud based HR systems, companies are investing heavily in programs to use data for all aspects of workforce planning, talent acquisition and management, and operational improvement. HR analytics has now become a business discipline, starting to provide new workforce insights, drive decisions about people, and improve business performance.

The benefits and use of HR analytics are compelling extending to:

- Identifying what is working well in various Business Units/parts of the organisation;
- Identifying those drivers that lead to improved performance and then focusing on strengthening those drivers;
- Identifying key workforce deficits and risks in particular groups or segments (e.g., low engagement or performance, high turnover or turnover risk);
- Developing targeted interventions to address those deficits and risks;
- Evaluating the effectiveness of past interventions (e.g., did recent salary increases to a particular workforce group or segment reduce turnover risk?).

Technology is a key strategic lever for HR to show its relevance and support the business objectives. The need for hard data on people has never been greater. This includes:

- Measurement of the impact and contribution of people/roles to business performance;
- Understanding the value contributed by various roles and workforce segments so as to drive more sustainable investment in people and organisations.

## 9.2 Ownership of HR Analytics

HR analytics has grown from a technical specialist group, to a serious business function that must meet the needs of many stakeholders throughout the company. Given this shift, there is a growing consensus that the best analytics programs are owned by a dedicated multidisciplinary group. Analytics involves a range of skills — from problem solving and data analysis to visualisation and statistics. Centralisation yields a stronger analytics result, with some organisations placing this in HR, while others have built a centre of expertise outside of HR.

## 9.3 Strategy Before HR Analytics

*The German philosopher Immanuel Kant once noted: 'theory without data is groundless, but data without theory is just uninterpretable'.*

To understand strategy, to operationalise strategy or to evaluate strategy, one needs analytics. Analytics provides answers to strategic questions. Unfortunately the great divide between Strategic Workforce Planning and HR analytics still exists. HR analytics should inform on strategy and not exist in isolation. Otherwise the right measures and data may not be collected and configured in an appropriate way to provide the necessary workforce insights.

Many organisations in a rush to adopt HR analytics and improve their reporting about people, are doing so without having first developed a comprehensive workforce strategy to underpin the analytics and reporting. It's akin to putting 'the cart before the horse' with these efforts being partially wasted, unable to realise the full potential of the new reporting. A strategic approach to data analysis is required to generate insights. Unless one knows what to look for, the data will only show the numbers.

## 9.4 Some Definitions: Metrics, Measures, Data & Analytics

In the interest of clearing up any misconceptions concerning the meaning of terms relating to HR analytics, the following definitions are provided.

### Metrics and Measures

*Metrics are defined as a system of standard measurement.*
*Measures are concrete, usually measure one thing, and are typically quantitative in nature.*

A metric refers to the actual reading on a measure at a given time. Metrics describe a quality and require a measurement baseline.

HR metrics are about reporting information on employees. Examples of HR metrics include:

- Efficiency (e.g., FTE numbers);
- Effectiveness (e.g., quality, % improvement); and
- Outcome measures (e.g., business results/impact: sales, productivity).

### Data Analytics and 'Datafication'

*Data are facts or pieces of information used to calculate or plan something.*

Data can be analysed and interpreted using statistical procedures. As such, there is a need to understand statistical concepts such as: reliability, accuracy, consistency, correlations, causality and predictability.

*Analytics is the systematic analysis of data.*

Analytics are an essential strategic tool that can directly impact financial results. Statistics can only be numerical.

*'Datafication' is a new term to describe the turning of an existing business into a data business.*

In HR, datafication refers to the use of HR analytics to understand more and more about people, HR practices and processes, and the linkages to financial outcomes. As referred to above, the datafication of HR is a leading business trend today.

## Big Data

*Big Data refers to extremely large and complex data sets that may be analysed computationally to reveal patterns, trends, and associations, especially relating to human behaviour and interactions.*

Much IT investment is going towards managing and maintaining big data to provide the insights to enhance business performance. Big data challenges include capturing data, data storage, data analysis, search, sharing, transfer, visualisation, querying, updating and information privacy.

However whilst the amount of data organisations can mine for information that is increasing exponentially, the application of big data to HR analytics and reporting is limited. In-house data sets are typically on a much smaller scale (i.e., 'Little Data') and there is a need to fully exploit this little data in the first instance.

## 9.5 Investment in HR Technology

**Evolution of Human Capital Management (HCM) Solutions**

> *HCM software is a set of practices associated with people resource management including workforce planning, learning management, performance management, talent management, recruitment and payroll. HCM helps modernise HR processes, driving compliance and control, whilst driving performance.*

In the 1990s, the failure of Customer Relationship Management (CRM) and Enterprise Resource Planning (ERP) solutions to cater to the various demands, such as recruiting, learning and training, and compensation management, led to the emergence of dedicated HCM solutions. A rise in demand among enterprises to improve workforce management and the growing demand for integrated high performance software has further added to the rise in the adoption of HCM solutions.

These HCM solutions:

- Help organisations in the effective monitoring and tracking of employees' performance and collaboration; and
- Facilitate employees real-time access to critical information (e.g., time and attendance, payroll, benefits, performance).

The advent of modern apps and the inclusion of modern mobility have enabled organisations to address employees requests immediately. Many organisations are deploying HCM solutions for enhanced employee satisfaction, engagement and experience.

The constant developments in HCM technologies such as integration of cloud and mobility, and the emergence of the IoT, has further leveraged vendors to offer superior solutions to improve organisational productivity in a cost efficient manner. Thus there are HCM vendors, cloud services providers, third party service providers and technology providers. The ability of HCM solutions to offer a cohesive central system for managing HR activities in the areas of network maintenance and internal customer service has been an important part of its growth strategy.

## Technology Integration Challenges

Technology is an enabler. It gives HR professionals more visibility and control over processes, including benchmarking. The HCM solution space has waffled between point solutions, platform deployments, and combinations of the two.

As indicated above, functionality in the HCM market is growing more diverse with end users now having a large array of options to understand labour costs and productivity. However these options are independent, causing usability and data at an organisational level to be fragmented, disconnected and dependent on separate solutions to bring it all together.

As these niche HCM solutions emerge, integration capabilities such as direct Application Programming Interfaces (APIs) and platform analytics are allowing different solutions to link together and share data for cross-referencing and complete data analysis at a senior management level. These strategic integrations are unifying HCM data sets into a data ecosystem comprised of all functionality enablers that might be deployed. This single HR database system serves as a single master employee record, providing a centralised, holistic view of all aspects of the workforce. With the emergence of stronger integration options, end users (both managers and employees) have more options than ever to explore best practices across a full breadth and depth of capabilities. Previously this data integration has constituted the biggest barrier to effective HR reporting and analytics.

As referred to earlier, business systems that are built should be based on a mobile-first design, as a mobile device is typically the first place employees look about matters that affect them.

## Mobile Device Ownership and Management Model Considerations

*Note. The following considerations have application across the whole organisation and are not confined to HR matters.*

There are several areas for consideration in planning an enterprise mobility and mobile applications strategy including:

- Development of a mobile governance policy;
- Development of a clear set of metrics and assessment criteria to determine the effectiveness of the mobile strategy;

- Confirmation of an ownership and management model for devices;
- A role audit of various employees to determine what device, data, application and connectivity access is required;
- Approach to the adoption of either a single or multi-operating system;
- The extensiveness of the ecosystem to support the application integration and mobility platforms;
- The suitability of various processes and workflows to be ported to a mobile environment;
- Mobile application development approach (i.e., either in-house or with third parties);
- Approach to mobile application use (e.g., internal use by employees or external use by customers);
- An audit of legacy systems and issues relating to their porting to mobile applications;
- Security issues relating to the device, the data and user, including a risk assessment of data accessed through mobile devices and applications;
- Containment approaches;
- An assessment of the importance of a mobile-first approach to applications;
- Approach to application development (e.g., hybrid, mobile web, or native applications) including application version upgrades;
- Integration requirements of mobile applications (e.g., with the IoT, other devices);
- Application user interface considerations (e.g., with smart phones, tablets);
- Any off-line storage of data and associated security considerations.

## IoT Strategy Considerations

There are several areas of consideration for organisations planning their IoT strategy including:

- Person(s) responsible for researching and evaluating IoT opportunities;
- Researching and discovering innovative IoT solutions and approaches;
- Adoption of an in-house IoT development approach or with a third party;

- Evaluating the success of IoT initiatives;
- An audit of IoT capabilities that encompasses internal resources and skills;
- Internal training programs and skills development requirements;
- Appropriateness of network architecture in place to deal with multiple IoT solutions;
- The mixed and fixed wireless connectivity required to support IoT solutions;
- Development of an IoT security program and guidelines;
- Appropriateness of mechanisms in place for compliance with licensing, data privacy and regulatory requirements;
- Managing, gathering and analysis of IoT data;
- Necessity of the provision of visibility and control of end-to-end management of the IoT platform;
- Approach to asset management of devices;
- Possible involvement of an edge computing approach within the IoT platform so that data sits where the user is;
- Importance of the deployment of IoT technology and its interoperability across other systems.

## Platform Analytics

The platform analytics engine sits underneath the HCM solution set, tying together databases produced by the individual solutions. While individual solutions run their own analysis of the data they collect, the platform layer amalgamates the data sets, converting them into a single language so they can be analysed as one entity within the platform layer, or exported back to individual solutions.

Platform analytics provides the analytics path to understanding the complexities of the workforce. Refer to Chapter 5.5 on further information concerning platforms.

## Data Correlation Challenges

Single sign on has provided a more seamless transition between different solution user interfaces and direct data correlation, but the concept of a single user interface across all solutions (i.e., CRM and ERP systems) remains a distant dream for many. The disconnected diversity means a lack of data continuity, with managers having to balance multiple views with this lack of unity. The future challenge is to connect HR data with business performance data, to bring together data from both systems and connect people to business results providing further strategic insights.

## Cloud-Based Technology

HR tech role outs are replacing legacy systems. The advent of cloud-based technology and solutions are enabling the movement of HR or workforce analytics up the maturity scale. Their use enables a reduction in time frame for organisations to get 'tech ready', with the first analytics up and running reduced to a few months, if not less. Also this cloud-based technology is consistent with the push to a single global core HCM solution to enable advanced HR analytics, more rigorous talent management, and better employee experience. Reference has been made earlier in Chapter 4.5 to the mindshift from one of ownership of resources to one of sharing of resources.

Primary benefits of 'the cloud' to HR typically include:

- Reduced physical infrastructure;
- 24x7 data accessibility from anytime, anywhere;
- Support of real time visibility of data;
- The ability to scale;
- Relief from having to maintain the necessary IT infrastructure and overheads; and
- Timely access to the latest updates and features.

The cloud does indeed have a silver lining.

Common drawbacks can involve:

- The deployment, usage and security concerns related to Service as a Software (SaaS) HCM solutions, including across mobile devices;
- A lack of complete control;
- The critical need to keep current with the latest release of updates and new functionality; and
- Assessing the value of upgrades and managing the same, including the associated outages.

In successfully moving complex platforms like HRMS to the cloud, there is a need to adopt a road mapping strategy, service delivery strategy, and change enablement. This moving will involve process and data integration challenges. As HR teams have adopted cloud-based technology, they have taken on responsibilities that were previously the domain of the IT department. This has caused HR to invest and seek candidates with advanced skillsets focused on cloud vendor management, data analysis and more. Refer earlier to HRs' extended role in digital transformation in Chapter 7.

## Technology, Data and Interpretation

Buying sophisticated technology to collect data is only the start: the data needs to be translated into a clear story before it becomes useful or actionable. Before investing in a new system, HR must be clear on exactly what they want to measure, and then how and when the information will be delivered to drive and deliver results.

## Software Tools: Performance Improvement, Engagement, Wellness and Assessment

The array of software tools available relating to performance management and improvement, engagement, wellness and assessment include the following.

1. Continuous performance management tools
2. Feedback and data driven engagement tools
3. Wellness and fitness tools
4. Learning experience and smart learning tools
5. Candidate tracking, analysis and sourcing tools
6. Social recognition and reward tools
7. Team productivity tools.

## 9.6 Implementing HR Analytics

**Four Key Challenges**

There are four key challenges in implementing HR analytics:

1. Most companies are riffled with inconsistent HR data, which wouldn't typically be the case for financial data (see below)
2. Data is in silos (i.e., not integrated), so there is a need to consolidate and/or integrate various workforce management systems into a cohesive integrated technology stack, towards a single source of truth!
3. HRs' well documented lack of analytical acumen and the ability to connect business results to data about employee performance, including knowing those employee metrics that have greater impact on business results, requires an understanding of data analysis and statistics
4. For the people using the new software, integrating its' use into their daily work.

**Data Policy and Governance**

The quality of data in HR continues to be a challenge as referred to above. A critical but sometimes unappreciated component of building a sustainable HR analytics capability is the creation of a governance data approach that includes consideration of the following:

- Responsibility for data management and policy;
- Development and implementation of a security and data protection policy, including firewalls;
- Addressing processes for standardisation and data legislation compliance;
- Data storage requirements;
- Maintaining software licensing requirements;
- Deploying enterprise wide definitions, formulas, hierarchies, maintenance and the like;
- Data access and privacy considerations;

- Data input including the associated training of staff;
- Data cleansing if new definitions are adopted;
- Data protection if it is required to be transferred.

# Chapter 10
# Conclusions

# 10  Conclusions

As indicated from the outset, this book is more about the people factor and less about technology. We have covered a broad range of issues, some in more detail than others. Also we have provided some background to explaining recent developments in the workplace in addition to providing a view of the future.

Digital disruption and transformation is evolving at an alarming pace. Transformation of the workforce – the way it is utilized, managed, and improved - is essential to digital transformation. We would argue that transformation of the workforce is also essential for the survival of those organisations that are less affected by digital disruption. As identified in the Preface, there are a number of factors and drivers causing many organisations to rethink how they may best manage their people.

Whatever the case, Strategic Workforce Planning is now a must have! The importance of the people factor still prevails, even more so. Furthermore, the above transformation can only be achieved by HR helping to create an agile organisation built on a collaborative culture that meets the demands of the business.

# References

# References

Alzheimers.net (2016). Retrieved from: www.alzheimers.net/resources/alzheimers-statistics

Beeson, M. (2017). The ROI of Digital Business Transformation. *Forrester Research.* . Retrieved from https://www.forrester.com/report/The+ROI+Of+Digital+Business+Transformation/-/E-RES91701

Benedikt, C., & Osborne, M. (2013). The future of employment: How susceptible are jobs to computerization? *Oxford Martin School, University of Oxford.* Retrieved from http://www.oxfordmartin.ox.ac.uk/publications/view/1314

Bersin by Deloitte (2017). *Learning organisational maturity – A quantum leap ahead for learning organisation maturity.* Retrieved from http://www.bersin.com/News/EventDetails.aspx?id=20872

Bersins by Deloitte (2017). *Create a new talent experience.* Retrieved from https://www.fuel50.com/2017/04/create-new-talent-experience/

Bersin, J., Flynn, J., Mazor, A., & Melian, V. (2017). The employee experience: Culture, engagement and beyond. *Global Human Capital Trends, 2017.* Deloitte University Press. Retrieved from https://dupress.deloitte.com/dup-us-en/focus/human-capital-trends/2017/improving-the-employee-experience-culture-engagement.html

Catlin, T., Scanlan, J., & Willmont, P. (2014–15). Raising your digital quotient. *McKinsey Quarterly, June 2015.* Retrieved from http://www.mckinsey.com/business-functions/strategy-and-corporate-finance/our-insights/raising-your-digital-quotient

Cariss K., & Vorhauser S. (2017). *Cliffhanger: HR on the precipice in the future of work.* Melbourne: PageUp People Ltd., Amazon.

CEB (2016). *The real impact of removing performance ratings on employee performance.* Retrieved from https://www.cebglobal.com/blogs/corporate-hr-removing-performance-ratings-is-unlikely-to-improve-performance/

CEB (2017). *Customer experience survey. CEB Customer Experience Leadership Council.* Retrieved from https://www.cebglobal.com/marketing-communications/customer-experience.html

Chesbrough, H. (2011). *Open services innovation: Rethinking your business to grow and compete in a new era.* Jossey-Bass.

Chui, M., Manyika, J., & Miremadi, M. (2015). Four fundamentals of workforce automation. McKinsey Global Institute. *McKinsey Quarterly, 2015.* Retrieved from http://www.mckinsey.com/business-functions/digital-mckinsey/our-insights/four-fundamentals-of-workplace-automation

CIO (2017). Retrieved from http://www.cio.com/article/3141994/it-strategy/a-new-digital-cio-must-emerge-from-digital-economy-disruption.html

CIPD (2017). *Employee Outlook: Focus on employee attitudes to pay and pensions: Winter 2016–17.* Retrieved from http://www2.cipd.co.uk/PM/peoplemanagement/b/weblog/archive/2017/02/28/half-of-older-employees-plan-to-work-past-65-says-cipd-survey.aspx

Davenport, T. & Kirby, J. (2016). *Only humans need apply in the age of smart machines.* HarperCollins Publishers (AU), Amazon.

Deakin University's *Graduate Learning Outcome 3 (DU GLO 3),* (2017). Retrieved from http://www.deakin.edu.au/library/teach/digital-literacy/elements-of-digital-literacy

Deloitte (2014). *Digital disruption short fuse, big bang? Building the lucky country 32, Building imperatives for a prosperous Australia.* Retrieved from https://www2.deloitte.com/au/en/pages/building-lucky-country/articles/digital-disruption-harnessing-the-bang.html

Deloitte Access Economics (2017). *Australia's digital pulse: Policy priorities to fuel Australia's digital workforce boom.* Produced for the Australian Computer Society. Retrieved from: https://www2.deloitte.com/au/en/pages/economics/articles/australias-digital-pulse.html

# References

Dichter, S., Gagnon, C., & Alexander, A. (1993). Leading organisational transformations. *McKinsey Quarterly*, February, 1993. Retrieved from: http://www.mckinsey.com/business-functions/organisation/our-insights/leading-organisational-transformations

Edgar, P. & Edgar, D. (2017). *Reinventing middle age.* Melbourne: Text Publishing Company.

Erikson, E. (1969). *Childhood and society.* Middlesex UK: Pelican.

Friedman, T. L. (2017). *Thank you for being late.* UK: Penguin Random House.

Galbraith, J. R. (2007). *The star model.* Retrieved from http://www.jaygalbraith.com/images/pdfs/StarModel.pdf

Gill, M., & Fenwick, N. (2015). The digital business imperative. *Forrester Research*. Retrieved from: https://www.forrester.com/report/The+Digital+Business+Imperative/-/E-RES115784

Gittons, R. (2017). A return to world trade's glory days appears unlikely. *The Age*, July 15, 2017. Retrieved from: https://robertbrain.wordpress.com/2017/07/15/15-july-2017-theage-a-return-to-world-trades-glory-days-appears-unlikely/

Gnanasambandam, C., Harryson, M., Srivastava, S., & Wu, Y. (2017). Product managers for the digital world. *McKinsey & Company*, High Tech, Article, May 2017.

Greenberg, E., Hirt, M., & Smit, S. (2017). The global forces inspiring a new narrative of progress. *McKinsey Quarterly*, April, 2017. Retrieved from: http://www.mckinsey.com/business-functions/strategy-and-corporate-finance/our-insights/the-global-forces-inspiring-a-new-narrative-of-progress

Gregersen, H. (2017). Innovative leaders make innovative companies. *MIT Leadership Centre.* Retrieved from http://leadership.mit.edu/innovative-leaders-make-innovative-companies/

Hagel, J., & Singer, M. (1999). Unbundling the corporation. *Harvard Business Review*, March-April, 1999. Retrieved from https://hbr.org/1999/03/unbundling-the-corporation

HBR, 2016, Accelerating the pace and impact of digital transformation. *Harvard Business Review*, Harvard Business Review Publishing, June 2016. Retrieved from https://hbr.org/sponsored/2016/11/accelerating-the-pace-and-impact-of-digital-transformation

Holiday, P. (2017). *Fit for the Future: The 5 stages of organisational innovation.* Retrieved from http://www.peteholliday.com/fit-for-the-future-framework/

Jaffre, A. (1963). *Memories, dreams, reflections of Carl Jung.* Toronto: Random House.

Kane, C., Palmer, D., Nguyen Phillips, A., Kiron, D., & Buckley, N. (2016). Aligning the organisation for Its digital future. *MIT Sloan Management Review and Deloitte University Press.* Retrieved from htpp://www2.deloitte.com.us/en/pages/technology/articles/mit-sloan-management-review-and-deloitte-digital-business-study.html

Korn Ferry (2016). *The right workforce today and tomorrow.* Retrieved from: https://www.kornferry.com/institute/the-right-workforce-today-and-tomorrow

Korn Ferry (2017). *Rebuilt to last: The Journey to digital sustainability.* Retrieved from http://infokf.kornferry.com/Digital-Sustainability-LP_Digial-sustainability-LP.html

Lunenburg, F. C. (2012). Organisational structure: Mintzberg's framework. *International Journal of Scholarly, Academic, Intellectual Diversity*, Volume 14, Number 1, 2012. Retrieved from https://platform.europeanmoocs.eu/users/8/Lunenburg-Fred-C.-Organisational-Structure-Mintzberg-Framework-IJSAID-V14-N1-2012.pdf

McCrindle Blog (2107). *Happy working in the gig economy? Depends whether it's a choice or forced.* Retrieved from: http://mccrindle.com.au/the-mccrindle-blog/the-gig-economy

Meister, J. (2017). *The Employee Experience is the Future of Work: 10 HR Trends for 2017.* Retrieved from: http://www.forbes.com/sites/jeannemeister/2017/01/05/the-employee-experience-is-the-future-of-work-10-hr-trends-for-2017/

Microsoft (2018). *Building Australia's future-ready workforce.* Retrieved from: https://enterprise.microsoft.com/en-au/articles/digital-transformation/building-australias-future-ready-workforce-2/

Perry, M. (2014). *Fortune 500 firms in 1955 vs. 2014. AEIdeas.* Retrieved from: http://www.aei.org/publication/fortune-500-firms-in-1955-vs-2014-89-are-gone-and-were-all-better-off-because-of-that-dynamic-creative-destruction/

Pillans, G. (2017). Learning – the foundation for agility and sustainable performance. *CRF Research.* Retrieved from: www.crforum.co.uk

Power, P. G. (2017). The five essentials of leadership. *InPsych* August 2017, 39 (4). Retrieved from: http://www.psychology.org.au/inpsych/2017/august/power?

Reimer, D., Feuerstein, H., Meighan, S., & Kelly, S. (2017). *It's time for a second playbook: HR's leadership role in transformation.* Retrieved from: https://www.linkedin.com/pulse/its-time-second-playbook-harry-feuerstein

Salt, B. (2017). Generation kipper is happy as a long-stay guest at hotel mama. *The Australian.* Retrieved from: http://www.theaustralian.com.au/news/inquirer/generation-kipper-is-happy-as-a-longstay-guest-at-hotel-mama/news-story/c5ab369442e76ffb59d0e6975c480f0e

Sundararajan, A. (2017). WorkMarket 2020 In(Sight) Report. *KRC Research.* www.workmarket.com

Saxena, S. (2016). *The rise of the chameleon worker.* Accenture. Retrieved from https://www.linkedin.com/pulse/rise-chameleon-worker-shashank-saxena

Schmidt-Subramanian, M., & Stern, S. (2016). *Why CX? Why now?* Retrieved from https://www.forrester.com/report/Why+CX+Why+Now/-/E-RES134521

Swisher, V., & Dai, G. (2014). *The agile enterprise: Taking stock of learning agility to gauge the fit of the talent pool to the strategy.* Korn Ferry Institute. Retrieved from https://dsqapj1lakrkc.cloudfront.net/media/sidebar_downloads/KF-Agile-Enterprise.pdf

TRA (2016). *Digital transformation: Are you disrupted or disrupting?* Retrieved from: https://www.telstraglobal.com/images/Disruption,%20digital%20transformation%20and%20effective%20technology%20strategy%20report.pdf

Ulrich, D. (2017). *Disruptions in HR that every pro should know.* Retrieved from https://www.linkedin.com/pulse/modern-disruptions-hr-every-pro-should-know-dave-ulrich

Vie, C. (2016). *Global digital workforce transformation through strategic workforce planning.* Retrieved from https://ieondemand.com/presentations/global-digital-workforce-transformation-through-strategic-workforce-planning

Appendix A

Other Recent Past Workplace & Workforce Developments

## A.1 Recent Workplace Changes

Prior to the emergence of 4IR, over the past three decades or so, we have witnessed unprecedented change sweeping the workplaces of the western world. A combination of factors has contributed to this revolution including:

- Economic reform, of which the recent Global Financial Crisis (GFC) was a significant part;
- Technological developments (including improved communications and information systems and greater connectivity between people with the boundary between the digital and physical worlds disappearing);
- Globalisation, with the world becoming smaller and more interdependent;
- The economic rise of South East Asia (including China and India) and Africa also emerging into the economic spotlight;
- Some western powers decelerating (e.g., some European countries);
- A greater concern for the environment and future generations (e.g., global warming);
- Increased emphasis on compliance and risk mitigation, particularly post the GFC;
- Changing social values (e.g., move towards individualism, people having a voice, greater independence, seeking deeper meaning);
- Greater (workforce) diversity in terms of age, gender, ethnicity, level of education, family status and personal ambition;
- An aging population with increased life expectancy and declining birth rates (i.e., the 'demographic crunch' of and ageing workforce and a shortage of talent with the pattern of life cycle predictability broken);
- Advent of the knowledge economy with the polarisation of skilled versus unskilled jobs and widening inequalities (i.e., shortage of talent and excess of labour);
- Increased customer demands (i.e., wanting more choices, 24/7 service);
- Shareholder demands increasingly being perceived to override employees' welfare.

Appendix A: Other Recent Past Workplace & Workforce Developments

It should be noted that shareholders are less loyal than employees, with the average shareholder tenure (according to Cascio, 2009), being around 12 months, compared to employees of around six years (i.e., average turnover of the Australian workforce is around 15%).

In the public sector, the volume and pace of administrative reform pursued by governments has been unrelenting with:

- A demand for improved efficiency in the delivery of quality services;
- Increased emphasis on accountability and transparency of transactions;
- Increased competition for resources and a demand to do more with less;
- Outsourcing, corporatisation, and privatisation;
- Greater customer focus, analysis of activity costs, and a recognition of community service obligations;
- An emphasis on equity, diversity, equal opportunity, etc.

The turbulent business environment has become more decentralised and information driven, with ever increasing diversity. Organisations need to be lean, fast and flexible in order to survive and remain competitive. In so doing, they have had to continually redefine themselves through cost cutting, restructuring, re-engineering, divestments, acquisitions, etc. They have become more demanding of higher levels of employees'/workers' performance in responding to increased customer demands, changing markets, products and technology.

## The Legacy of the Global Financial Crisis

In addition to the above, the Global Financial Crisis (GFC) has left, and will continue to leave, an indelible footprint on many organisations that include, amongst other things:

- An increased focus on assessing and mitigating risk;
- More stringent corporate governance;
- Consolidation, with a greater emphasis on long-term value creation and sustainability, given lower growth rates.

## A.2 New Meanings in the Workplace

New workplace meanings have emerged from these changes, some of which have been referred to later in the 'new deal' (refer to A5). These meanings include the following:

- The traditional notions of employment and careers have changed, as have the characteristics of organisations, the workplace, and the needs of individuals;
- Some concepts such as 'job security' are fading and have been replaced by the notion of 'employability';
- The term 'management' has acquired a new significance, with an increased emphasis on influence, strategic considerations, co-ordination, integration, facilitation and support, and a reduced emphasis on authoritarianism and control;
- Traditional boundaries between organisations and customers have become blurred (e.g., formation of alliances), with both employees/workers and organisations now coming in many shapes and sizes;
- Work restructuring and more flexible arrangements, including the delocalisation of work, has given many employees/workers the task of managing their own work;
- The death of the old eight hour work day being an anachronism of the industrial age;
- Widespread changes in education levels (with an increased emphasis on professionalism), and work related values such as autonomy and responsibility, have also emerged with restructuring.

Work and careers have now become more of a series of employers and learning opportunities, rather than a life-long relationship with one company until death (retirement) do us part!

As has been referred to earlier, with recent developments in technology, new channels of communication have been opened up and business models transformed in some industries, creating new services and jobs. These developments have also facilitated the outsourcing of work, including outsourcing to overseas (i.e., global labour mobility), and an increase in the number of home workers.

> **Note.** *Globalisation means that supply chains can be located across the globe with markets becoming increasingly international. The pool of skilled labour that employers can potentially draw upon has expanded greatly.*

## A.3 Organisational & People Management Trends

These trends or changes have been separated into two broad categories:

1. Changes to how organisations are operating;
2. Changes in people management practices.

### Organisational Trends

These trends include:

- Flatter hierarchies with the outsourcing of non-core activities;
- More fluid forms with the formation of alliances, networks, project based teams, team based structures and virtual organisations;
- An emphasis on organisational agility and faster response times and an ability to innovate;
- The development of service oriented cultures;
- A concern for sustainability, Corporate Social Responsibility and the triple bottom line beyond a sole focus on short-term profits.

### People Management Trends

These trends include:

- An emphasis on competitive advantage in the recruitment and retention of capable and valued employees, and in particular employer branding, talent management, succession planning and workforce planning;
- An increased emphasis on leadership and coaching, and the development of 'soft skills' (e.g., emotional intelligence), as being seen to be critical to effective leadership, management and performance;
- A demand for higher performance and skill levels;
- A preference for experience of new hires over internal development;

- A requirement for managers to have deeper knowledge (either industry or subject areas) plus people skills;
- The abandonment of the traditional employment relationship (i.e., the paternalistic 'old deal') with greater complexity in managing employer/employee relations;
- The adoption of employment strategies that are designed to share more of the risks with employees/workers (e.g., adoption of shorter-term contracts and recourse to a contingent workforce of contractors, casuals, part-time employees and consultants).

*Note.* Economies based on advanced manufacturing and services require different forms of work organisation, combining greater individual autonomy with new forms of collaborative teamwork.

## A.4 Changing Employment Practices

As referred to above, many organisations of all sizes and industries reviewed their employment strategies in order to remain competitive. Consequently a variety of employment relationships have spawned. There has been a shift towards:

- Fixed-term contracts;
- Greater use of casuals;
- More project based work;
- More flexible work practices, such as part-time, job sharing and telecommuting;
- Greater use of contractor/consultant alternatives;
- Outsourcing of various activities (typically non-core activities or lower knowledge/lower skill activities);
- Offshoring of labour with lower cost and more fluid global labour markets.

There has been a strong downward trend in the percentage of people in full-time permanent jobs, particularly post the GFC. In essence, the more flexible employment practices adopted have created shorter-term arrangements and higher externalisation, resulting in reduced job security and less predictability in employment relationships.

Furthermore opportunities are now more readily able to import knowledge and expertise, including diversification and expansion through the establishment of alliances, virtual organisations, access to consultants and contractors, etc. Notwithstanding this increased flexibility and risk minimisation, organisations are also vitally concerned with:

- Preserving (or attempting to increase or optimise) employees'/workers' commitment and performance;
- Developing a positive corporate culture;
- Attracting, engaging, developing and retaining valuable people and their skills, including key talent and those in more critical roles.

The traditional employer/employee model is progressively being replaced with other arrangements, with the phenomena of labour hire agencies growing. Organisations now need to 'have their cake and eat it' in terms of the flexibility and commitment of their workforce (refer later to Chapter 21).

*Note. Most studies show that contingent workers are just as committed to the organisation they work for as permanents, and generally they are willing to act in the interests of the organisation. However retention of contingent workers is more problematic as their barriers to exit are lower.*

This move towards the externalisation of employees (i.e., workers) reflects the shift by organisations away from a reliance on social exchange considerations, to more of a reliance on economic exchange considerations. The end result is that employees/workers are now taken on as calculated risks. This shift has implications for:

- Employees/workers in managing their careers, investing in their own skills' development, and taking greater control over their own destiny;
- Organisations in terms of the development and retention of skills to maintain their competitive advantage.

## One Size Doesn't Fit All!

Overall employment relationships have become more diverse, individualised, implicit, deregulated, decentralised and generally more tenuous and transitory. Employees now come in all shapes and sizes! As such, it is clear that a 'one size fits all' approach to workforce management will no longer suffice.

Dealing with this complexity implies a need for differentiation which raises new challenges for management, including:

- Maintaining traditional notions of equity, against the background of labour market forces (i.e., supply and demand for skills), resolving tensions between permanents and contingents, and catering for the needs of various demographic groups (e.g., Gen Y and X, Baby Boomers);
- Replacing outdated concepts and models with contemporary mindsets and more sophisticated frameworks and models in rethinking and determining workforce strategies.

## A.5 The 'Old Deal' & the 'New Deal'

### The 'Old Deal'

Loyalty has been considered essential for survival in the past where belonging and being part of a community was necessary for survival. And so it was the case in the workplace with the paternalistic relationship between employer and employee that existed up until the late 80's—referred to as the 'old deal' between employer and employee.

This 'old deal' was based on the straightforward exchange of job security (and financial security), promotion and advancement, and material rewards, for loyalty and service, with employees prepared to move around (i.e., to locations as required by the employer). It was largely implicit and unquestioned, and assumed homogeneity of employees' requirements.

Whilst the 'old deal' provided certainty, stability, and a sense of place and purpose in one's class structure, it may well be argued that it also created a form of blind loyalty and dependence that inhibited performance, initiative, risk taking and willingness to change. To some extent it required the willing sacrifice of the employee's sense of and desire for freedom, to the higher demands of the organisation, with subservience to command and control.

However when loyalty is demanded, accountability becomes diffused! As indicated earlier, the organisational change revolution that began in the 1980s with mergers, acquisitions and downsizing, sent a clear and unforgiving message that organisations could and would only be loyal to individuals while it suited their purposes—only while economic circumstances enabled them to afford it.

## Characteristics of the 'New Deal'

So if the paternalistic 'old deal' is dead, what has replaced it? What is the 'new deal' employment relationship that has emerged over the past three or more decades? Essentially the 'new deal ':

- Is more exchanged based (i.e., what's in it for the employee/worker as well as what's in it for the organisation), and of shorter-term duration;
- Incorporates new employee/worker attitudes and values;
- Incorporates clarified mutual expectations, responsibilities, understandings and commitments between organisations and their employees/workers.

    More specifically, 'new deal' employment relationships typically:

- Are less paternalistic (i.e., more 'arms length');
- Are characterised by greater flexibility (including a tolerance for role ambiguity and change), mobility (i.e., of shorter-term duration), openness and self-reliance/autonomy;
- Should be built on the basis of adult-adult attitudes and responsibilities, trust and cooperation;
- Incorporate a more mature form of commitment (i.e., to the vision, values and goals of the organisation, as opposed to 'blind loyalty');
- Incorporate a greater employee/worker involvement and 'voice' in what is going on;
- Foster the career prospects for higher knowledge/skill and valued employees, where 'employability' is emphasised rather than job security;
- Need to balance short and long term considerations;

- Are more performance based, where what counts is the current value that employees/workers contribute;
- Emphasise quality working relationships (e.g., teams, customers, suppliers, alliances);
- Incorporate a recognition and an understanding of the continually changing needs of both parties.

However no one 'new deal' will provide the ultimate collaborative solution given the:

- Diversity of the nature of industries, organisations and the environments in which they operate;
- The value that various levels or groups of employees/workers contribute;
- The needs and interests of various demographic groups and individuals.

## A.6 'New Deal' Implications

### For Organisations

Clearly organisations now have much more flexibility in terms of how they are able to configure and manage their workforce. Having a workforce that is accessible, skilled, motivated and efficiently deployed will increasingly be a key differentiator of business performance and financial success. However this increased flexibility may have come at a cost to both parties: employers and employees/workers.

The loss of employees'/workers' job security has weakened their attachment to employers, leading to reduced incentives for employer funded training (apart from key talent). Long-term commitment by employees to the organisation has been replaced by greater attachment to their careers. The conundrum for employers is that by promoting the concept of employability, they have encouraged employees to focus on the market and direct their attention outside of the organisation.

## For Employees

Employees are therefore continually re-evaluating their existing 'deal', the benefits of working for their current employer, and their career progression. This conundrum has been exacerbated in recent times with the growth of search firms and the increasing propensity to 'poach' talent.

Some workers have become more of 'free agents', whose loyalty is predominantly to them. They have taken advantage of the autonomy, freedom, flexibility and new career choices that the contemporary workplace has to offer. Their attachment to particular organisations has become more tenuous as they seek 'employability' (i.e., development of their knowledge, skills and experience), rather than employment. In short, they have learnt to use the organisation that they are with to achieve their own ends.

# A.7 Workforce Diversity & Three Generations

The three pillars of diversity are:

- Age;
- Gender; and
- Ethnicity.

In this section, we shall deal only with age and generational cohorts. This is not to diminish the importance of both gender and ethnic diversity.

With regard to age diversity, values and beliefs do vary across generations. This is to be expected with each generation affected by the social, political and economic circumstances of its time. The question is to what extent these differences are real or imagined. And then the second question is what are the implications for organisations in terms of how they may manage these differences?

Given the high importance that some attach to this issue with regard to the development of workforce strategies, these generational differences are elaborated upon below.

## Perceived Generational Differences: Pop Psychology?

It is contended that some of these perceived generational differences and the social diversification of our four generational workforces are over emphasised. They can be better explained within a framework of human development, where people go through various stages in the life cycle, each with different challenges (e.g., from teenagers, young adults, middle age, etc.). An American psychologist Erik Erikson (1969) described the various psychological stages that a person goes through in growing up with his developmental model over the life span (refer Appendix B).

In any event, a more sophisticated analysis of, and approach to workforce strategies is required, rather than simply just appealing to perceived generational differences.

## Generational Boundaries Artificial

The workforce has become more multi-generational in terms of age. Unfamiliar managerial challenges are emerging, associated with all age cohorts in the evolving workforce mix, all with different wants and needs. We shall focus on three age and career cohorts:

- Gen Y or Millennials (1980–1996);
- Gen X (1965–1980); and
- Baby Boomers (1946–1964).

These generational boundaries are somewhat arbitrary, having been artificially created for the sake of simplicity. Gen Z (1997 onwards) has not been considered as many would only have recently commenced employment.

One should therefore be careful to avoid stereotypes, and assume that perceived generational characteristics apply to particular individuals—these generational groups are not homogeneous (refer to Baby Boomers later). Notwithstanding and as alluded to above, people learn, work, interrelate and even think as a consequence of the culture, dominant events, technology and educational methods of their formative years. Therefore it is useful for employers to understand the generational mix of their workforce and how different cohorts may be more likely to behave and interact.

Appendix A: Other Recent Past Workplace & Workforce Developments

## Gen Y (Born from 1981) or Millennials

Most Gen Y employees are not amenable to accepting organisational practices and decisions that are not advantageous to them and their careers. They:

- Are demanding substitutes for job security that include competitive rewards, opportunities for learning and career progression and being treated with respect;
- Value a more collegiate workplace and democratic participation;
- May be more heavily cause motivated;
- May prefer not to work with a large organisation;
- May prefer to work with an organisation where the mission statement and culture aligns with their personal beliefs;
- Have a more entrepreneurial disposition, being interested in starting up their own businesses;
- May be more self-sufficient having experiences the effects of the GFC;
- Work more to live (i.e., require flexible work practices), as opposed to the reverse, so work may not necessarily be as important in their lives.

Of all of the cohorts, they appear to be unhappiest in their jobs and less satisfied (Dytchwald, Erikson & Morison, 2006), possibly because they are still finding their place in the world. Contrary to popular notions, statistically it would appear that younger employees 'job hop' not too much than their counterparts did 20 years ago.

## Gen X (Born from 1965 to 1980)

Like Gen Y, Gen X seeks:

- More immediate and competitive rewards (both extrinsic and intrinsic);
- Job challenge, opportunities for learning and skill development, career development, support, autonomy and equitable treatment.

More flexible work practices are important to some (e.g., those with family responsibilities), but not to others.

## Baby Boomers and More Mature Aged Employees/Workers (Born from 1946 to 1964)

Older employees/workers have different motivations for working with some:

- Needing to work for financial reasons;
- Simply enjoying working and are not yet ready to retire
- Wanting to give something back, to make a difference or make a meaningful contribution (i.e., leave a legacy).

Research indicates that around:

- One third of older employees/workers wish to keep on working beyond the eligible retirement age;
- One third are looking to work part-time (not necessarily in the roles to which they are currently engaged); and
- Another third are seeking to stop work altogether.

However this is a changing mix with the aftermath of the GFC and the erosion of superannuation provisions and increased life expectancy.

Flexibility is a key theme in supporting their retention, including options around work schedules and location. Most research converges on the conclusion that work content that provides intrinsic challenge and satisfaction for older employees/workers may be the core element in any successful strategy for dealing with such career concerns as plateauing and the downsized organisation. Increasingly, mature aged employees/workers are interested in pursuing worthwhile projects, developing new goals and interests, which signal their entering a period of new beginnings.

Thus we are witnessing a new shape to the careers of older employees/workers. For businesses competing for skills, there is a clear value in retaining capable and experienced staff for longer, and in smoothing management transitions. Furthermore as Boomers represent a very large group of customers, companies may also benefit from ensuring the profile of their front line staff broadly aligns with their customer base.

Appendix A: Other Recent Past Workplace & Workforce Developments

## Generational Differences Overcooked?

As alluded to earlier, generational differences may well be over emphasised. It is contended that we have much more in common than we have differences, whatever our age. For example, most people are looking to:

- Do meaningful work and make a contribution;
- Work with an organisation that they can identify with;
- Work for a supportive boss and with a supportive team;
- Be recognised and adequately for their efforts;
- Be provided with adequate resources;
- Have open communication with their employer concerning workload, performance targets and other matters that are likely to affect them.

Hudson research (Levy, Carroll, Francoeur & Logue, 2006) on the perceived differences between Gen Y and Gen X concluded the following:

*Both crave gentle direction and pat on the back feedback from sensitive but strong leaders who seek to engage their staff. This study debunks popular theories that Gen X and Y are different and require different management approaches to allow them to flourish.*

Nevertheless one should be careful in assuming that various groups are seeking the same benefits for the same reasons. For example, on the subject of flexible work practices, the three age cohorts all want flexible work practices but for different reasons:

- Young people want time to explore things outside of work (e.g., travel);
- Mid-career employees/workers want time for family and community;
- Mature aged employees/workers want to pursue other interests outside work (e.g., recreation, volunteering, travel, etc.).

Finally a further word of caution on the tendency towards stereotyping individuals according to perceived generational differences. For example, there is a danger of:

- Blaming turnover on generational differences rather than looking within at the true causes;
- Assuming to know the desires and aspirations of individuals based on what demographic group they may belong to (i.e., there is a need to drill down to understand these desires and aspirations at an individual level).

## Other Groups with Particular Needs

Beyond the above three generations there are other groups each with particular needs including:

- Single adults without dependent children;
- Working women with young children trying to balance career and domestic responsibilities and demands;
- The 'sandwich generation' (i.e., intergenerational dependency) caring for elderly parents as well as a young family;
- Older workers whose careers may have plateaued, with careers growing longer (with increased life expectancy) and having to cope with the anti-age bias.

The clear conclusion from all of the above is that there is a need to treat people as individuals—to better connect with them, to identify their wants and needs, and where it suits both parties; to address and try to meet those needs.

# A.8 Overall Implications & Challenges for Organisations

Based on the above discourse, the implications and challenges for organisations have been summarised below:

- The need for their workforce to be flexible and to adapt in a volatile environment;
- Greater workforce diversity with organisations having to reckon more with the needs of various demographic groups (e.g., Gen Y, Gen X and Baby Boomers, Sandwich Generation, etc.);
- Structuring and managing a variety of employer/worker relationships in an increasingly complex workplace, consistent with the needs of the business;
- Fostering of citizenship commitment amongst employees/workers and a sense of community;
- Maintaining organisational coherence and some semblance of internal equity, given the polarisation between skilled and unskilled jobs, and the different workforce strategies applicable to these two groups (e.g., reward mechanisms, flexible work practices, etc.);
- Further maintaining internal equity with the rise of market influences and the disruptive effect on internal salary structures and relativities due to fluctuating supply and demand for various skills;
- Building commitment in new ways and enhancing performance (i.e., doing more with less) and retention of skills (particularly for those in more critical roles);
- Maintaining trust with their workforce, against a background of uncertainty, rapid change, greater demands and flatter structures (i.e., 'walking the talk' with organisational rhetoric);
- Greater vulnerability in terms of the labour market (i.e., not just competing locally), with opportunities to import labour;
- Greater demands on managers, employees/workers, some of whom need to be accessible 24/7 given customer service standards are constantly increasing;
- Accommodating a variety of needs generally of their employees/workers and connecting better with individuals;

- Providing for changing work/career needs of people over the employment life cycle, and assisting/supporting employees in their career development, ongoing education and transitions;
- Continuously competing for talent (i.e., attraction, development and retention of talent), with 'poaching' of talent on the increase (with the growth of search firms);
- Balancing autonomy with control, particularly with flexible work practices and managing a remote workforce;
- Keeping pace with technology and managing the associated risks;
- Responding to increased community sensitivities concerning the environmental and social impacts of their business activities.

## A.9 Overall Implications & Challenges for Individuals

Implications and challenges for individuals include the need to:

- Cope with and adapt to change, including handling transitions;
- Develop 'soft skills', including relationship building, greater self-reliance and resilience;
- Balance work and family demands;
- Add value and perform consistently well;
- Take charge of their own career, and self-manage it through different stages and cycles;
- Commit to ongoing learning and invest in their on-going training and skill development.

# Appendix B
# Stages of Life

## B.1 Erikson's Stages of Life

The American psychoanalyst Erik Erikson (1969) felt that the social problems encountered in the course of development were more important than the biological ones. He described a progression of psychological stages in which the child faces a wide range of human relations as he/she grows up. According to Erikson, all human beings pass through a series of major crisis with each stage as they progress through the life cycle. At each stage there is a critical confrontation between the self the individual has achieved thus far, and the various demands posed by his/her social and personal setting. A failure to resolve a particular stage crisis means that 'baggage' may be carried through until perhaps a later resolution.

If we look at Erikson's proposed stages from adolescence, through to early adulthood, to middle age and then later years, he sets out these development tasks appropriate to that stage and the psychosocial crisis of that stage.

### Erikson's Eight Stages Of Man

| Approximate Age | Development Task at that Stage | Psychosocial Crisis of that Stage |
| --- | --- | --- |
| 0–1½ years | Attachment to mother, which lays foundations for later trust in others | Trust versus mistrust |
| 1½–3 years | Gaining some basic control of self and environment (e.g., toilet training, exploration, tying shoe laces) | Autonomy versus shame and doubt |
| 3–6 years | Becoming purposeful and directive | Initiative versus guilt |
| 6 years to puberty | Developing social, physical and school skills | Competence versus inferiority |
| Adolescence | Making transition from childhood to adulthood; developing a sense of identity | Identity versus role confusion |

Appendix B: Stages of Life

| Early Adulthood | Establishing intimate bonds of love and friendship | Intimacy versus isolation |
| Middle Age | Fulfilling life goals that involve family, career and society; developing concerns that embrace future generations | Productivity versus stagnation/self-absorption |
| Later Years | Looking back over one's life and accepting its meaning | Integrity versus despair |

In particular for middle age, the development task proposed is 'fulfilling life goals that involve family, career and society: developing concerns that embrace future generations'. The psychosocial crisis of that stage is 'productivity versus stagnation' (i.e. there is an absence of a sense of growth and the alternative is stagnation and decay). Now Erikson talks about the 'mid-life transition' in adult development in which the individual reappraises what he/she has done with her life thus far (i.e. what is happening in relationships with partners, relatives and friends, including a re-evaluation of his/her marriage, career, lifestyle etc.).

This is also a period when the individual begins to see physical changes as the biological clock ticks away; changes that show 'the summer of life is over and the autumn of life has begun' (Jung, as in Jaffre, 1963). There is a shift in the way one thinks from 'How long have I lived?' to 'How much time do I have left?' One starts to become aware of one's own mortality!

# B.2 Jung's Theory of Individuation

Carl Jung (Jaffre, 1963) was a Swiss physician, whose theory of human development is based on the process of moving towards fulfilment of the unique potential within each of us, hence the term 'individuation'. Jung had a view of life which emphasised growth and change over the lifespan.

Now the first half of life, according to Jung, is one of accommodation—we adapt to the world. For instance, we identify with individuals, groups and organisations, and our roles amplify who we are. We develop a persona or mask that enables us to develop stable and reliable ways to interact with others.

However our persona can also hide who we are. We can become over identified with certain roles. For example, stereotypes of the pinstripe suited lawyer or the staid accountant are examples of occupational roles that come to mind. During this first half of life, we are preoccupied with our career and possibilities, and perhaps have lost touch with the important hidden properties of our nature. According to Jung, our goals up until this stage have been mastery and achievement of the outside world.

So having an 'external' orientation in the first half of life, Jung contends that the second half of life has a more internal orientation, concerned with the search for:

- Individual identity;
- Self-authenticity;
- Self-actualisation;
- Achieving a sense of integration or wholeness.

At mid-life we begin the transition of turning inwards, which for some people may mean a 'crisis'. So in a sense, this crisis represents a compensatory mechanism, which enables us to develop neglected aspects of ourselves. An imposed loss such as the experience of organisational change, redundancy or job loss, may act as an external trigger precipitating such a crisis. Alternatively there may be internal triggers to do with the personal circumstances of the individual that precipitate such a crisis, for example:

- Divorce;
- Death of a friend or family member;
- Loss of youth/health;
- Unfulfilled dreams, hopes and ambitions.

In summary, we have seen that adulthood or mid-life can be viewed as a stage of our growth and development as a person. As in the case of other stages of life (refer to the Erikson model presented earlier), there are certain challenges that need to be faced, and changes or adjustments that need to be made, that for many may constitute a crisis. Erikson talks about developing concerns for others and fulfilling goals in terms of family, career and society, whilst Jung talks about finding ourselves.

# Appendix C

# Careers in the Contemporary Workplace

## C.1 The Traditional Career Model

Careers are an important part of who we are. An individual's career has a major impact on their life. As referred to earlier, under the 'old deal' employment relationship between employer and employees (that operated up to the mid to late 1980s), employers virtually guaranteed job security and assumed the major responsibility for an individual's career. In return, employees provided loyalty and service to the employer. The traditional or old career model was characterised by:

- A series of upward moves with steadily increasing power, status and income, where organisations were structured like pyramids;
- Employees staying in one career with 40 years uninterrupted work, sometimes with the one organisation (which was typically rewarded with a presentation of a gold watch on retirement at 65 years of age);
- Employees moving through one cycle of discrete career stages (e.g., exploration, establishment, maintenance, and decline);
- A continuous and relatively stable process where people had a single career identity;
- Career development being more the responsibility of the organisation.

However the paternalism and dependency that characterised the industrial age is no longer applicable. Under the 'new deal' employment relationship that is more 'exchange based' (i.e., what's in it for the employee as well as what's in it for the organisation), career management has now become much more the employee's responsibility. The rungs on the corporate ladder have become broken or obsolete! The career ladder has been replaced in part by a career lattice.

In today's turbulent workplace, some jobs/occupations have almost disappeared, whilst new ones have emerged. New career possibilities with seemingly previously unrelated combinations of disciplines, now constitute viable career paths (e.g., Law and Information Technology).

The ability of organisations to compete is predominantly vested in their people. Organisations therefore need to energise and retain their key talent and valued employees, who are critical to the success of the enterprise. Some critical career management questions include:

- What does the concept of a career mean in the contemporary workplace, given flatter organisational structures and no long-term guarantees?
- How much responsibility should the organisation take for the career development of their employees?
- What are some of the key career challenges that employees are facing in the contemporary workplace?

## C.2 New Career Models

On average, an individual will have between two to three career changes, and seven to nine jobs over their working life. Given that the old career model is relatively obsolete:

- What has replaced it?
- What is the new career model?

Of course the structured career continues to exist—characterised by career paths with stepped progression or pre-determined exposure to various work experiences. However this is now one of a number of forms of career models/types in the contemporary workplace including.

- The portfolio career: characterised by multiple jobs (some of which may be happening simultaneously) and employers, and plasticity (i.e., reskilling, reinvention);
- The open career: with career journeys characterised by project work, active internal mobility, and individual development;
- The spiral career: a combination of vertical and lateral career moves and life experiences;
- The flexible career: with career paths loosely defined, that can be varied according to individual circumstances;
- The boundary-less or portfolio career: a series of interwoven projects, patchwork of contracts/activities, where a person's career is not 'bounded' by an organisation;

- The protean career: the adaptable career (Proteus was a Greek god who could reinvent himself and adapt to any situation);
- The hyphenated career: where a person's work life may be interrupted by periods of unemployment or 'time out' for family or other personal reasons;
- The internal career: a person's perceptions and self-constructing of their career, where the importance of career script and psychological success (pursuing one's own purpose, goals and values and a search for inner meaning and connectedness), is emphasised.

All of the above models involve a more holistic concept of careers—looking at the whole person and their career within their total life: not just in terms of their occupation.

## C.3 Implications of New Career Models for Employees

The implications of new career models for employees typically include the following:

- Assuming greater responsibility for their career management and development (we are all self-employed!);
- Coming to terms with issues of self-definition (who am I?) and normlessness (what are the rules?), particularly for older workers who have grown up under the old career paradigm;
- The need for personal identity development and strengthening (one's identity is no longer so closely tied to the organisation);
- Development of career sub-identities (with dual qualifications and/or multiple occupational identities and/or industry associations);
- The possible need for frequent reinvention.

In short, employees need to take more responsibility for their career, develop new 'career mindsets' and develop more of an inner focus. Career growth is now one of self-actualisation or self-fulfilment of:

- Doing one's own thing and following one's own destiny;
- Developing one's own 'personal compass'.

Career development now requires a commitment to lifelong learning given the rapid explosion of new knowledge. However it may be difficult to balance time for learning against the demands of the job and/or the family or other responsibilities. Careers may need to be built both across and within organisations—staying too long may erode employment value! Career diversity is now much more valued in the contemporary workplace, and 'employability' has now become much more important than employment! Job security:

- Now lies more within the individual;
- Is not so dependent upon the organisation;
- Is a readiness and willingness to adapt!

Thus these changes in meaning and emphasis to the terms 'careers' and 'career development' pose significant personal development challenges and demands for many employees. Career development is no longer a 'one off' event following completion of secondary education (which involved making a choice and the completion of initial training or education), but rather a life-long process.

## C.4 The New Worker & Careers

### Surviving and Thriving

Just as organisations have been reinventing themselves in order to 'survive and thrive', employees/workers have been undergoing a similar process of reappraisal. This process has involved:

- A questioning of traditional beliefs and values;
- The shift to a more internal focus;
- A reappraisal of abilities, interests and attributes;
- Development of new understandings and adoption of contemporary career models (including associated career expectations and attitudes);

- Enhanced self-awareness and understanding;
- A strengthening of self-identity and purpose.

The demands of the contemporary workplace require a 'new kind of worker': one who is better equipped to manage a complexity of career and workplace issues, and deal more effectively with psychological pressures (whether their origin is from inside or outside of the workplace).

However development is a two-way responsibility. Some workers may decline or be unable to take up the challenges of the contemporary workplace. They risk being left riding in the 'white water turbulence'!

## How Organisations Can Assist

Organisations can play a part in assisting their employees to make sense of what is happening in the contemporary workplace. Implicit in this approach is an understanding of the drivers of recent workplace change, the dynamics of the contemporary workplace, and effective adaptation and coping strategies. The development of 'soft skills' needs to be reinforced, including:

- Self-responsibility;
- Proactivity;
- Perseverance;
- Relationship building;
- Resilience or hardiness;
- Flexibility and adaptability;
- Innovation;
- Continuous learning;
- Self-marketing skills.

Studies have shown that one of the key reasons for employee dissatisfaction is a lack of career options and self-development. Organisations can partly combat this by offering career self-development programs, so that individual career success and performance are optimised. Such an arrangement constitutes a learning partnership between the organisation and the employee.

## Benefits for Organisations

Apart from the need for employment relationship alignment, there are other organisational benefits in addressing the 'deeper' or 'soft skills' development needs of employees, including:

- The increased requirement for self-discipline and self-sufficiency with the delocalisation of work;
- The need for self-regulation in the workplace, given the prevalence of flatter structures without formal hierarchy;
- A required emotional display and self-management of feelings, particularly in customer service roles.

Personal development includes an emphasis on:

- Interpersonal and relationship building skills;
- Developing resilience;
- Handling change and ambiguity;
- Enhancing general life skills, all of which are transferable to any job/ career (i.e., development of 'soft skills').

The development of self-management and self-reliance skills reduces management load. Converging theories of work motivation emphasise the critical influence of volition and self-influences on performance. A person with a strong sense of mastery and high level of optimism is likely to approach change in a positive way, and is likely to exhibit a high level of work commitment, even in the face of uncertainty.

# C.5 Implications of New Career Models for Organisations

The role for organisations in the career development of their people has now become one of more support and assistance. This may typically involve:

- Providing access to career development knowledge, resources and techniques (including, where appropriate, online services, independent professional career guidance and coaching, etc.);
- Training and development on themes such as resilience, transitions, etc.;
- Encouraging continual learning in the form of training and development (including recognition of external studies);
- Fostering a career management and development ethos in the organisation (which may involve typical career pathing prospects, regular career development discussions where the continually changing needs of both parties can be reviewed, etc.);
- The accommodation of a variety of career needs of employees (consistent with the needs of the business).

However in the era of flatter structures, management is sometimes unsure as to what they are able to offer their employees by way of career development. Some employees are also unsure of what the concept of a career means in the contemporary workplace, given that the traditional career model is dead! Consistent with this approach is the need for organisations to:

- Develop potential career paths within the organisation;
- Provide cross-functional learning opportunities;
- Have a clearly defined training and development policy.

# C.6 Implications of New Career Models for Managers

Most managers have a responsibility to develop their people. Furthermore, career management and development constitutes the central theme of individual development. It therefore follows that basic career dialogue/counselling skills should form an essential or core management competency. However for managers to assist and develop their people, they need to be confident about their own career management and development. A manager who is unsure about his or her career direction, training and development needs, challenges, etc., is hardly in a position to assist his or her subordinates. Managers therefore need to:

- Have a deeper appreciation/understanding of what constitutes a career in the contemporary workplace, the issues and challenges facing employees, and the attributes required to 'survive and thrive';
- Have worked through their own career management and development issues;
- Demonstrated the personal qualities that contribute to a climate of trust and openness with their subordinates;
- Manage change and transitions effectively (given the constantly changing workplace);
- Manage a variety of relationships with their people;
- Have developed some basic skills towards engaging and assisting others in their careers.

One of the outcomes of the above support, assistance and relationship building, is a more engaged and satisfied workforce.

Appendix D

# The AWS Skills-Based Workforce Segmentation Model, Questionnaire & Plotting Tool

# D.1 About Critical Roles

## The Critical Role Identification Problem

There is no universal agreement on what constitutes a Critical Role in an organisation. Most organisations are lacking in an underlying model and methodology for identifying such roles. The result is that 'gut feel', influence and/or politics fills the gap!

Yet the identification of such roles is fundamental to succession planning and strategic workforce planning. It is these roles that impact more significantly on business outcomes and the achievement of the business strategy. Consequently they should attract a greater focus and higher levels of investment to maximize the ROI of HR initiatives.

Boards also want to know which are the Critical Roles in the organisation from a succession planning and risk management perspective.

## The Role of Agility

Agility plays a central role in the organisation of the future. It is dawning as the new organisational paradigm as the race to replace structural hierarchies with networks of teams empowered to take action accelerates. With such flatter structures it becomes less clear as to the value that various roles contribute to the strategic imperatives and business outcomes of the organisation.

## Linking Talent to Value

Role importance or criticality is closely linked to an explicit perspective on the value that can be created or enabled by role. **Understanding value and how it is created, is essential to adopting a value centric talent-management approach. Reallocating talent to the highest value initiatives is as important as reallocating capital.**

The potential rewards of value-based role clarity may even be greater in agile organisations because flatter organisations build themselves around the principle that empowered talent in the right roles is the key to unlocking value.

## Comparison of Roles

The SSQ allows roles with different levels, types of responsibilities and impacts, to be compared on a common metric, according to the value that they (a) create and/or (b) enable. This workforce segmentation tool provides a basis for targeted investment in various roles (i.e., according to their value generating importance and uniqueness), and also informs on the appropriateness of organisational structures (refer to page 4 of the brochure for further information and applications).

> *Note. The SSQ is not simply a job classification tool. It has much wider value and implications relating to the business strategy how an organisation manages its workforce. It requires a different mindset in thinking about roles and together with the associated plotting tool and compilation of the Role Analysis Report, is only available through consultancy input provided by AWS.*

## The Problem of Hierarchy

Hierarchy heavily influences which roles are viewed as most important in an organisation. Making decisions on top talent based on hierarchy results in a disconnect between value and talent. Not all roles on the same hierarchical level are of equal importance, create equal value, or contribute equally to the business strategy and outcomes. There is a need to understand the deeper characteristics of roles.

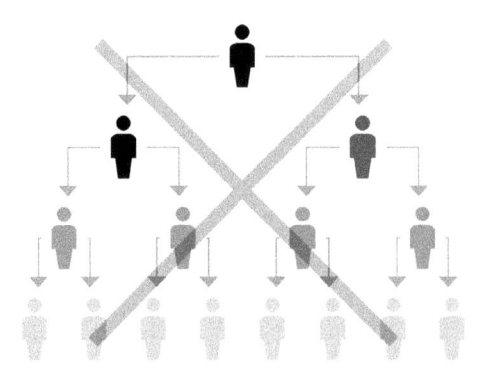

An excessive focus on hierarchy results in an underinvestment in some roles and an overinvestment in other roles. In any event, hierarchical structures are on the slide with the shift towards matrix accountability and network organisations. Furthermore, segmentation by job families or clusters suffer from the same above deficiencies.

### Job Families – A Cul-De-Sac!

Furthermore, segmentation by job families or clusters lead to a cul-de-sac or a 'road to nowhere', with little strategic value. This approach mixes 'apples with oranges', as there is no capacity to differentiate between 'Make' versus 'Buy' versus 'Critical Roles' all of which may form part of the one job family. Depending upon this role classification, different HR policies and practices, different EVPs, and different cost of turnover multiples should apply (refer page 4).

## D.2 About the Skills Segmentation Questionnaire (SSQ)

### What is the SSQ?

Advanced Workforce Strategies (AWS) has overcome the blind spots and limitations of identifying Critical Roles with the development of the Skills Segmentation Questionnaire (SSQ) and associated role plotting tool.

The SSQ is a 52 item questionnaire based on a workforce segmentation model that has been adapted from the work of Lepak and Snell (1999, 2002). It takes into account two dimensions of skills in analysing various roles – both their value and uniqueness to the organisation.

Appendix D

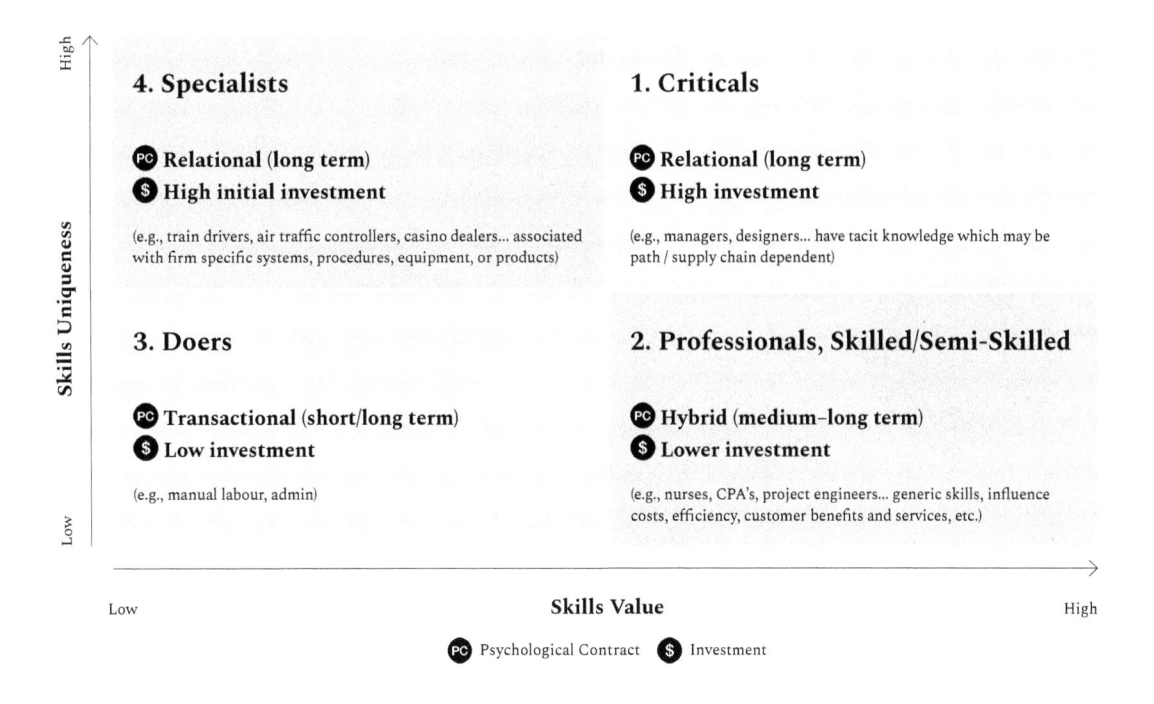

```
High │
     │  ┌─────────────────────────────────┬─────────────────────────────────┐
     │  │ 4. Specialists                  │ 1. Criticals                    │
     │  │                                 │                                 │
S    │  │ (PC) Relational (long term)     │ (PC) Relational (long term)     │
k    │  │ ($) High initial investment     │ ($) High investment             │
i    │  │                                 │                                 │
l  U │  │ (e.g., train drivers, air       │ (e.g., managers, designers...   │
l  n │  │ traffic controllers, casino     │ have tacit knowledge which may  │
s  i │  │ dealers... associated with firm │ be path / supply chain          │
   q │  │ specific systems, procedures,   │ dependent)                      │
   u │  │ equipment, or products)         │                                 │
   e ├──┼─────────────────────────────────┼─────────────────────────────────┤
   n │  │ 3. Doers                        │ 2. Professionals, Skilled/Semi-Skilled │
   e │  │                                 │                                 │
   s │  │ (PC) Transactional (short/long  │ (PC) Hybrid (medium-long term)  │
   s │  │      term)                      │ ($) Lower investment            │
     │  │ ($) Low investment              │                                 │
     │  │                                 │ (e.g., nurses, CPA's, project   │
     │  │ (e.g., manual labour, admin)    │ engineers... generic skills,    │
     │  │                                 │ influence costs, efficiency,    │
     │  │                                 │ customer benefits and services, │
Low  │  │                                 │ etc.)                           │
     │  └─────────────────────────────────┴─────────────────────────────────┘────▶
        Low                        Skills Value                          High

              (PC) Psychological Contract    ($) Investment
```

## About Valuable Skills

Valuable skills fall into two categories:

1. Creating
2. Enabling

The AWS Skills Value Framework is depicted in the diagram below. Roles are assessed in terms of their:

- Level of decision making in these various values (directly responsible or support function); and
- Impact (either localized or widespread) throughout the organisation.

Various roles may incorporate one or more of these values, both value creation and value enablement. It is important to understand the relative contribution or composition of that value generation.

**Value Creating**

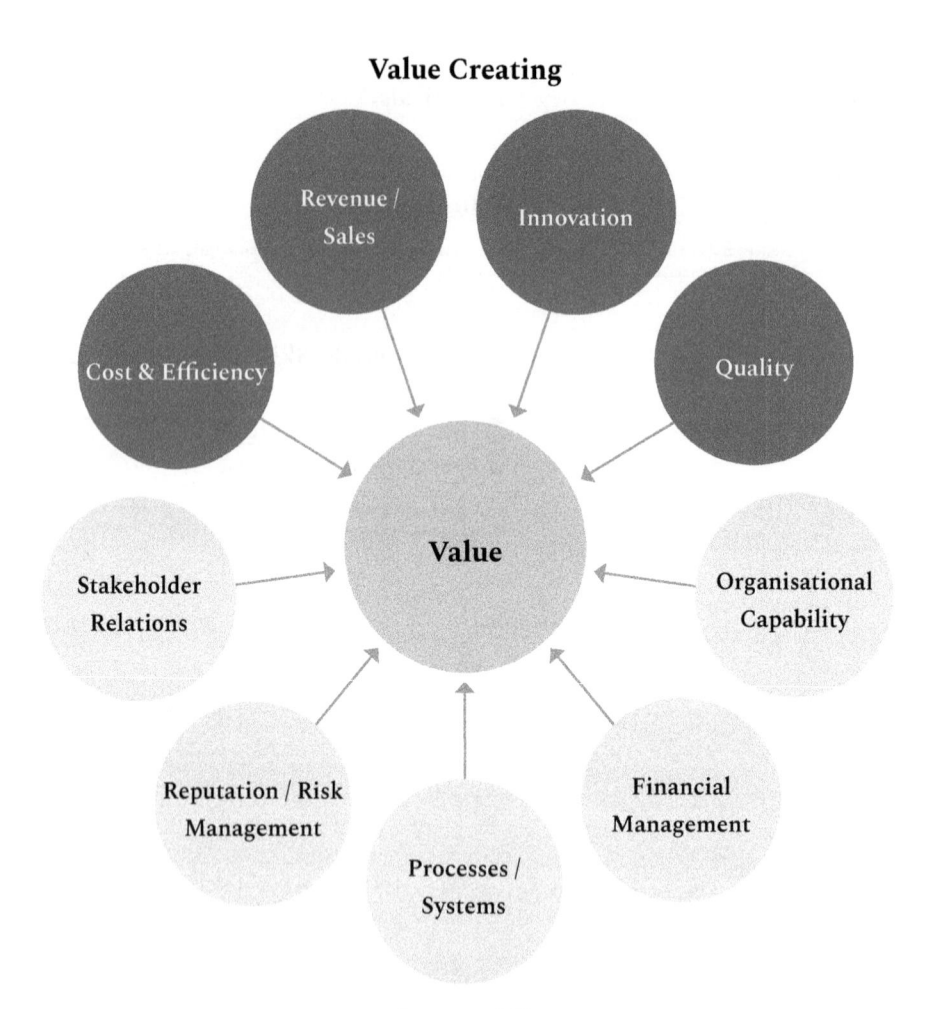

- Revenue / Sales
- Innovation
- Cost & Efficiency
- Quality
- Stakeholder Relations
- Organisational Capability
- Reputation / Risk Management
- Financial Management
- Processes / Systems

→ **Value**

**Value Enabling**

## About Unique Skills

Unique skills are organisational specific, unlikely to be found in the open market, hard to replace, and hard for competitors to imitate or duplicate. These skills need to be nurtured over time, given that they are not developed and acquired overnight. Hence organisations are more likely to invest in the education, training, and development of these skills.

## Fundamental Workforce Strategy Questions Answered by the SSQ

Whilst many organisations may have bundles of HR policies, and undertake workforce planning, succession planning and talent management, this is very different from having developed a whole of workforce strategy.

Appendix D

The outputs from the SSQ (i.e., classification of roles) provide answers to the following key workforce or human capital strategy questions:

- What really are the critical roles in your organisation?
- What roles should you 'make' by developing people from within? (Roles in quadrants one and four)
- What roles should you 'buy' people ready-made from the market? (Roles in quadrants two or three)
- What roles should you consider outsourcing? (Potentially roles in quadrants two and three)
- How should psychological contracts and attraction (including Employment Value Propositions/'Deals'), engagement and retention strategies, and levels of investment in L&D differ for the various types of roles/quadrants?
- What is the cost of turnover of the various types of roles?
- What is the state of succession planning for Critical Roles and Ultra-Critical roles:
    - Number of roles where successors are available now?
    - Number of roles where successors are likely to be available within the next 1 to 3 years?
    - Number of roles where there are no successors?

The focus of the SSQ role analysis is external, as opposed to the internal relativity focus of typical job evaluation models. It provides a basis for:

- Understanding the deeper characteristics of roles (including classification of role types);
- How and where roles create value; and
- Linking the importance of roles, and their impact on, the delivery of products and services.

Thus the SSQ facilitates the development of new workforce insights and understandings. It is fundamental to strategic workforce planning and forms the basis for reporting human capital data for the organisation (i.e., reporting data by the four quadrant model).

# D.3 Analysing and Plotting Roles

## Example of Various Plots

Various jobs within an organisation can be analysed with the SSQ according to the extent that they incorporate one or more of the above nine values, and also their impact (e.g., localized or widespread).

They can then be plotted according to four possible employment roles or quadrants. The following is an example plot of various roles.

You will note that Critical roles have been further segmented into Ultra Critical and Critical roles and similarly for Professionals. This more fine grained delineation provides even greater clarity relating to role importance and facilitates more insightful HR data analysis and reporting.

*Note. The final positioning of plots for these roles will vary according to the responsibilities of the roles and various organisational circumstances.*

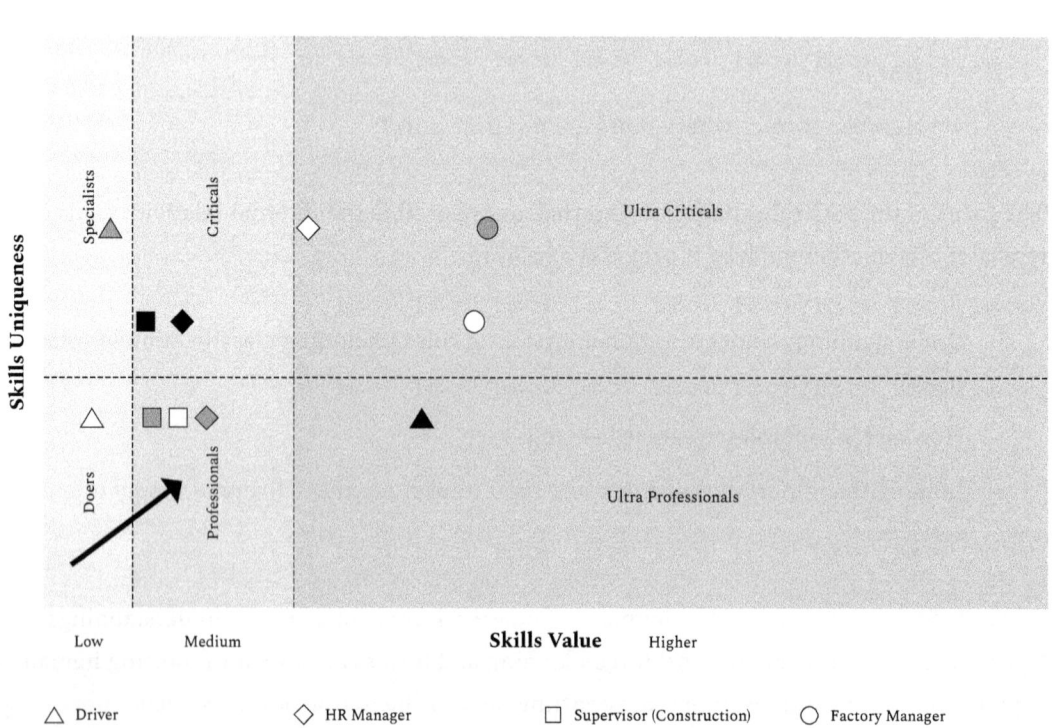

**Skills Workforce Segmentation Plots**

| Symbol | Role | Symbol | Role | Symbol | Role | Symbol | Role |
|---|---|---|---|---|---|---|---|
| △ | Driver | ◇ | HR Manager | ☐ | Supervisor (Construction) | ○ | Factory Manager |
| ▲ | Technician | ◆ | Teacher | ■ | Nurse | ● | CFO |
| ▲ | Journalist | ◆ | Biz Dev Manager | ■ | Sales Person | | |

## Linking Roles to the Business Strategy

There is also opportunity to weight the importance of the nine skills values on these plots, according to the business strategy. For example, if the business strategy is to improve the quality of its products, then any role that incorporates quality will attract a higher overall value score. Thus the SSQ facilitates the further linking of roles more closely to the business strategy.

With digital transformation, value enabling roles are now assuming greater prominence. For example, the previous backroom roles of HR and IT are now emerging as front and centre in the digital workplace because of the importance of these two value generaters in this transformation:

- Organisational capability (because of the changing shape of the workforce and the role of HR); and
- Processes/systems (with digitization and the role of IT).

## Linking the SSQ and EVPs

The SSQ and plotting tool can be used in conjunction with the Employment Value Proposition (EVP) Profiler. Different EVPs (i.e., mix of tangibles and intangibles based on the concept of the psychological contract) will apply to each of the four skills' quadrants. Thus this combination enables a strategic approach to determining the importance of roles and their respective HR policies and practices, investment in L & D, recruitment approaches, cost of turnover, etc. Refer to the EVP Profiler brochure on the AWS website.

The AWS has also developed a number of other tools based on the AWS Skills-Based Workforce Segmentation Model including:

- A cost of turnover calculation tool;
- A recruitment/redundancy forecasting tool;
- A legacy workforce tracking tool.

Refer to the AWS website for further details.

## SSQ Role Analysis Report

The output of the SSQ is the compilation of a Role Analysis Report for the classification of the various roles analysed including their plots.

The SSQ and associated Report is available from Advanced Workforce Strategies.

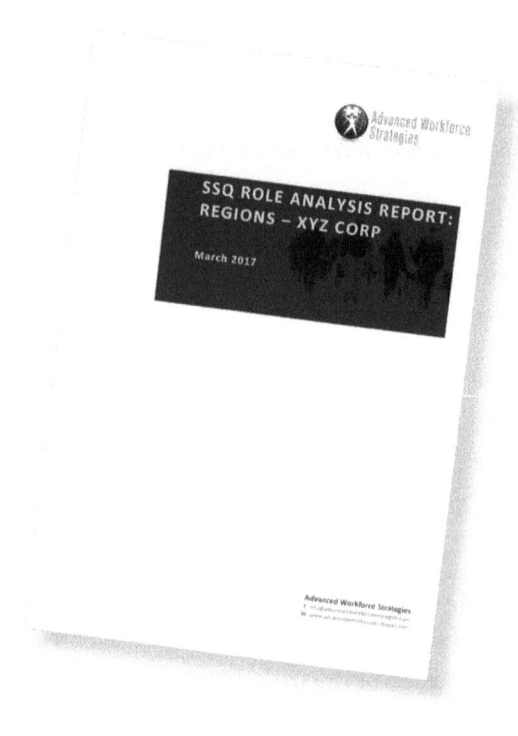

# Appendix E
# Other Publications

# Book: Aligning Workforce and Business Strategies: Mobilising the 21st Century Workforce

The alignment of business and workforce strategies is a "hot" topic in the HR and business domain. Many HR thought leaders and HR professionals have identified this as a key issue for those seeking to extract maximum value from their most important intangible asset – their people.

This book provides a road map for those seeking to achieve this alignment. It firstly explains what is meant by a workforce strategy, as opposed to workforce planning. Then a three layered model of organisational critical capabilities, core competencies and individual job competencies of the firm is introduced from which the strategy of the business can best be conceived. The focus is then on strengthening these capabilities and competencies by identifying their underpinning key drivers.

These drivers are in turn integrated with a new skills' based approach to segmenting the workforce, analysing and differentiating roles, including the identification of critical roles. Limitations in the traditional approach to segmenting the workforce on a hierarchical/job level basis, and job evaluation basis and job family basis are exposed. Those roles that are more closely linked to these key drivers then assume greater importance and focus (including associated levels of investment) in order to maximise the performance of people in those roles.

Other themes that are addressed in this book include workforce configuration, outsourcing, psychological contracts, engagement and retention, brand and Employment Value Propositions, measurement and reporting of HR data (including workforce analytics and the tree categories of HR data).

This book is available for purchase from the AWS website.

# White Papers

- Identifying Critical Roles;
- How to Avoid the 12 Deadly Traps of Strategic Workforce Planning;
- The 9 Key Steps in Digital Workforce Transformation;
- Adopting a Value-Centric Agile Approach to Talent Management;
- Enhancing Organisational Agility and Customer Centricity.

These white papers are available for download from the AWS website.

# About the Author

**Colin Beames**

Managing Director, Advanced Workforce Strategies
B.Eng, BA(Hons), MBA
Corporate Psychologist

Colin Beames is a business focused organisational psychologist (and formerly a civil engineer), author and thought leader in human capital, Strategic Workforce Planning (SWP) and digital workforce transformation, with a deep and expansive knowledge of these subjects.

Prior to his mid-life career change from civil engineer to organisational psychologist, Colin held senior management roles in the concrete, quarrying and mining industries. His fourth year Bachelor of Arts honours psychology thesis was on the topic of mid-life career change and his subsequent Master of Business Administration (MBA) thesis was on developing an engagement and retention diagnostic survey tool—the Workplace Relationship Development Indicator (WRDI)—based on the concept of the psychological contract.

He is now the Managing Director of Advanced Workforce Strategies, a firm that provides consultancy services in the areas of SWP, workforce segmentation and configuration, measurement and reporting of human capital, workforce engagement and retention surveys (including key talent risk assessment), and organisational development/ business reviews.

To that end, he has adapted and integrated various models based on recent research in the area of SWP, including the development and application of associated tools. These include the AWS Skills-Based Workforce Segmentation Model for identifying Critical roles, 'make' roles, 'buy' roles, and a model for profiling Employment Value Propositions (EVPs) based on the psychological contract.

Colin has presented SWP workshops internationally (including the UK, South Africa, South East Asia, New Zealand) as well as throughout Australia. He has consulted to organisations both in the public and private sectors and he has previously written and published two books.

His recent clients include the following:

- Commonwealth Superannuation Corporation ($45 billion worth of investments);
- 13Cabs/Cabcharge (Australia's largest taxi company);
- RMIT University, Melbourne (90,000 students): One of Australia's largest universities;
- Celcom, Kuala Lumpur (4,500 staff): One of Malaysia's largest mobile phone network service providers;
- Methanex, Canada and New Zealand (1,500 staff): The world's largest supplier of methanol with eight large manufacturing plants globally.;
- Telekom Malaysia, Kuala Lumpur (30,000 staff): Malaysia's largest telecommunications company with international operations;
- IAG, Sydney (15,000 staff): Large Australian based insurance company with South East Asian operations;
- Bank of South Pacific, Port Moresby (3,000 Staff): Largest bank in the South Pacific with 78 branches throughout the region;
- Thomson Reuters, London (40,000 staff): The world's leading source of intelligent information for businesses and professionals;
- Other SMEs include: Cabrini Health, MS Queensland, various Local Government Agencies in Victoria.

# Client Testimonials

### Corporate Research Forum, London, SWP Workshop, 2015

Colin Beames is a global thought leader in Strategic Workforce Planning. The 1 day workshop that he designed and facilitated on this topic was over subscribed and attracted a record attendance for our workshop events with over 170 participants registered. These participants included HR Directors, Executives, Managers and Professionals from major UK national and global firms.

The rich content presented in this workshop was significantly more advanced than typically what currently has existed on this subject—it is truly 'cutting edge'. Colin has cleverly combined a number of research based human capital models into an integrated and holistic package that addresses the challenges of contemporary workforce strategy management and planning.

He has given the term 'strategy' a deeper meaning by adding substance to the rhetoric of strategic workforce planning and aligning workforce and business strategies. Colin also has exposed the limitations of some traditional approaches and models in strategic workforce planning with the introduction of his AWS Skills-Based Workforce Segmentation Model and emphasis on understanding the characteristics of roles.

He was able to fully engage and stimulate his audience over the day by his presentation style, and use of case studies and activities that illustrated the application of his strategic workforce planning approach, all of which consolidated the learnings. This resulted in one of our most successful events.

I would unreservedly recommend Colin Beames and the AWS Strategic Workforce Planning approach to any HR senior professional seeking to become more strategic, more business focused, exert greater impact on their organisation, and to manage their workforce more effectively.

*Mike Haffenden, Director, Corporate Research Forum*

## Thomson Reuters, London, SWP Workshop, 2015

Colin Beames ran a workshop on Strategic Workforce Planning for approximately 15 of our very senior HR professionals during his UK visit in 2015. This workshop was well received and stimulated lively interest and discussion amongst our group. In particular the AWS Skills-Based Workforce Segmentation Model that Colin has developed offers some new insights and understandings on roles including the identification of Critical Roles. Combined with a number of other human capital models and their application, Colin has taken Strategic Workforce Planning to a heightened level of thought leadership and sophistication.

By using Colin's methodology to sharpen our focus on Critical Roles and combining it with retention risk analytics, we were able to increase retention of this key population (VP and above) from 85% to 99% in one year. Using even the most conservative estimate of 100k per person cost of loss that equated to GBP1.5m of savings in one year. A more realistic estimate to include cost of replacement, loss of productivity, loss of knowledge would put the saving closer to GBP10m.

*Richard Cleverly, Global Head of Talent and Development at Thomson Reuters*

## HR Society, London, SWP Workshop, 2015

Colin Beames has developed some unique models for holistic approaches to Strategic Workforce Planning. These include the identification of those roles in an organisation that are strategically critical. He has developed presentation, analytical and interactive materials that form a sound and professional platform for engaging workshops and internal consultancy. Together with his excellent books, he has established himself as a global expert in this field.

*Andrew Mayo, Professor of Human Capital Management at Middlesex University*

## SIOP and SABPP, Johannesburg, SWP Workshop, 2016

In a recent workshop offered in Johannesburg, South Africa, Colin Beames shared a wealth of knowledge regarding Strategic Workforce Planning, to a local audience of senior professionals from various industries. Colin was able to impart his knowledge and experience in a palatable manner and in doing so affected the participants ranging from creating an appetite for SWP to deepening the levels of understanding of more seasoned professionals.

Besides the very valuable knowledge sharing that took place, this event also created the opportunity for SIOPSA (Society for Industrial and Organisational Psychology in South Africa) together with SABPP (South African Board for People Practices) to collaborate in hosting an event and in doing so opening the door to future similar collaborating.

*Lourens van Schalkwyk, Head: SIOPSA Academy*

## Celcom, Kuala Lumpur, SWP Consultancy, 2014

I worked closely with Colin Beames when he was recently engaged by Celcom in Kuala Lumpur to advise the organisation on issues of Strategic Workforce Planning, workforce segmentation and reconfiguration. Colin interviewed all of the senior executives and ran workshops for both the Managers and HR professionals as part of an education and training program for those groups.

After having searched the market to determine what other consultants offer, I found Advanced Workforce Strategies' models and thought leadership to be truly 'cutting edge'. Using the AWS Skills-Based Workforce Segmentation Model, we were able to gain some very valuable workforce insights including developing strategies and interventions towards addressing some labour management issues. This resulted in some significant labour cost savings for the organisation, as well as paving the way for out-of-the-box workforce solutions.

*Iqbal Hassan, Head HR Strategy & Analytics, Celcom Axiata Berhad*

## Large Insurance Firm, Australia & South East Asia, SWP and Digital Disruption Consultancy, 2017

In our firm undergoing digital workforce transformation, we spoke to many consultants concerning their service offering in Strategic Workforce Planning. There was one company that was a stand out: Advanced Workforce Strategies (AWS). In particular their AWS Skills-Based Workforce Segmentation Model and Skills Segmentation Questionnaire (SSQ) has allowed us to analyse and view roles from a new perspective, and better understand our legacy workforce.

*Matthew Coleman, Organisation Architect, Enterprise People & Culture, People Performance & Reputation*

advancedworkforcestrategies.com

Ingram Content Group UK Ltd.
Milton Keynes UK
UKHW020735100423
419916UK00009B/450